Sex—Let's Talk About It

by

Wendy Treat

Harrison House
Tulsa, Oklahoma

06 05 04 03   10 9 8 7 6 5 4 3 2 1

Sex—Let's Talk About It
ISBN 1-57794-557-3
(Formerly ISBN 0-931697-53-0)
Copyright © 2001, 2003 by Wendy Treat
P.O. Box 98800
Seattle, WA 98198

Published by Harrison House, Inc.
P.O. Box 35035
Tulsa, Oklahoma 74153

Dedication

To my husband.

I like being yours.

I like you being mine.

Table of Contents

1

God Made Sex, and It Was Good

When we enter a marriage relationship, we come with everything we've been taught, everything we've experienced, perceived, decided, denied, and buried. We come with much good, but we also bring a lot of baggage.

This baggage is loaded down with all the wrong ideas we've collected and developed over the years. These wrong ideas consist of the vows we've made because we've been hurt, fears we've adopted because we didn't understand, and the conclusions we've drawn from wrong information.

This baggage, this wrong thinking, makes us draw incorrect conclusions about sex and causes us to behave in ways that cheat our spouse and ourselves out of the good God has for our marriage.

At least once a week, my husband, Casey, and I receive calls at our church from people considering divorce and needing help. Year after year, as we minister to these men and women, I'm constantly reminded of how important sex is to any marriage. These callers are not divorcing over sex, but the quality of sex and what it represents in their marriage plays a major role in the quality of their marriage.

It makes all the difference in their marriage when a husband and wife truly understand how to give themselves to each other, how to be vulnerable to one another and enjoy good sex.

Consequently, couples without a great sex life need to find out what's wrong and make changes. When they allow God to heal what's broken in their hearts, He can fix what's broken in their thinking.

When my husband and I were dating more than 25 years ago, I had a small Toyota. It was a great little car that took me everywhere. I had a very busy schedule and didn't know anything about cars. Casey and I both attended Bible school, taught youth church, attended numerous services, and Casey taught on the radio.

One day a dashboard warning light came on in the car. I was not sure what it meant, but after a couple of days it went off.

I immediately felt relieved and thought, *Great! The Lord healed the car.*

Wrong.

Within a week, my little car was dead. It didn't need healing; it needed resurrection. The transmission fluid had drained completely out. The cost for repair was more than the value of my car; it was history.

It wouldn't have been very hard to put some transmission fluid in my car. But why didn't I do it? Why didn't I take a few simple steps instead of waiting until it was too late, and the car engine was all burned up?

I learned a valuable lesson from that little light on the dash and have carried it over into many areas of my life, including my marriage.

I believe there's a "flashing light" on the forehead of our spouses. It goes off for a while, and we think, *Whew. Everything's okay. The light's out.* But all we have really done is move from "low on fluid" to "burned up."

I don't want that for my marriage, and I don't want it for yours. For years, women have come to me and asked the most significant questions regarding the intimate parts of their marriages. Many of those questions have been about sex.

There is such a need among women to be liberated—to know the freedom of good sex and to cherish this gift God has given to married couples.

God wants us to have a great marriage. That includes every aspect of our relationship—public and private.

Among the tough questions I've answered about marriage relationships, I found that the core questions, though varied by individual circumstances, are all similar. They encompass heart-wrenching longings to understand and really know:

- Why do I have to have sex at all?
- How many times a week should we have sex?
- He wants me to wear things I'm not sure I want to wear.
- She wants to have sex before we marry. I don't want to hurt her, but I want to wait.
- She says oral sex isn't really sex. Is that true?
- It hurts that I had past relationships. How can I forget them?

And on and on the questions continue.

God Himself has already answered all of our questions. His Word is truth (John 17:17) and is full of His wisdom, mercy, and love.

As you take a journey with me through the pages of this book, we'll explore the answers to the questions above and many more. As you read I encourage you to allow God's truth to transform your thinking as well as your sex life. Your spouse will love the change, and so will you.

It is time for Christian couples to expose wrong thinking and believe what is right. It's time to pay attention to the "warning light." The truth is that God made sex, and He made it good. He gave it to husbands and wives as a gift. I like to call it a celebration of love because that's the essence of it. Whatever you call it, God wants you and your spouse to have a great sex life *all* your married life. He wants you to enjoy it from the toes up.

A Wedding Gift From God

When God created man (Adam), the Bible says that God created him both male and female. (Gen. 1:27.) And when Adam named all the animals as recorded in Genesis 2, Eve was part of him. Let me explain what that means.

After Adam named all the animals, he realized there was no one for him.

> So Adam gave names to all cattle, to the birds of the air, and to every beast of the field. But for Adam there was not found a helper comparable to him.
>
> GENESIS 2:20

God quickly took care of that. Genesis 2:21-23 tell us that Eve "was taken out of Man" by God and given to Adam as a partner:

> And the LORD God caused a deep sleep to fall on Adam, and he slept; and He took one of his ribs, and closed up the flesh in its place.
>
> Then the rib which the Lord God had taken from man He made into a woman, and He brought her to the man.
>
> And Adam said: "This is now bone of my bones and flesh of my flesh; she shall be called Woman, because she was taken out of Man."
>
> GENESIS 2:21-23

In reality, Eve was taken out of the side of Adam. The Hebrew understanding communicates that she was part of Adam.[1] (v. 22 AMP.) God literally took from Adam's flesh to form Eve. Then He brought them together as a husband and a wife.

The importance of this understanding is that man and woman—together—are whole. They are one flesh and one spirit. One is not elevated over the other. There are differences, but one is not better than the other.[2] Both are essential. One is not complete without the other. I have heard it said that in God's original design, the masculine/feminine attributes were one.

God never intended men to be with men or women to be with women in an intimate sense. (Rom. 1:26-32.) God never intended a woman to be with her boyfriend or a man to be with his girlfriend intimately. God created a man to have a wife, not wives, and a woman to have a husband, not husbands. His original plan was for one husband and one wife to be complete with each other.[3] Hebrews 13:4 says, "Marriage is honorable among all, and the bed undefiled; but fornicators and adulterers God will judge."

Fornication is two unmarried people having sex with each other. Adultery is voluntary sex between a married person and someone other than their mate. In the truest sense, sex is for a husband and a wife, and no other combination. Remember, God has called it "honorable" and "undefiled." It's good to be married. There is nothing unspiritual or unclean about the marital sexual relationship. God doesn't turn His head when you and your mate have sex. He doesn't turn out the lights or say, "Oh no, there they go again."

He made sexual intercourse for marriage, and it is undefiled. I believe it is as clean as worship to God; it's as pure as reading your Bible. It's part of life. God gave you the necessary physical body parts and the desire, so He's not shocked when you use them. He isn't in heaven wondering where you came up with the idea. He gave you the idea.

Religious, uptight, negative thinking from incorrect information has caused shame concerning sexual relations in marriage, and the price has been that too many Christians have damaged or lost their marriages over sex.

Joined by God

The act of being "one flesh" was created for marriage. God called Eve Adam's wife. (Gen. 3:17.) She was not his girlfriend, date, or one-night stand. There is a big difference between a woman and a wife and how a man responds to each. Genesis 2:24,25 KJV gives us the program:

Therefore shall a man leave his father and his mother, and shall cleave unto his wife: and they shall be one flesh.

And they were both naked, the man and his wife, and were not ashamed.

In *The New King James Version*, verse 24 reads: "Therefore a man shall leave his father and mother and be joined to his wife, and they shall become one flesh."

The word *joined* means to connect or bring together, to combine, to become a member of, to unite with, to become connected with.[4] In short, we are to be one with our mate. God joined the man to his wife.

When couples marry, it is so important for them to realize they are joined. They no longer belong to Mom and Dad. They are not to bring Mom and Dad into their issues. The man and the woman joined in marriage are to cleave to one another and leave Mom and Dad.

If a husband or wife feels bound to what their parents want them to do, then they have not left their parents. If a wife feels bound to obey her parents and not join her husband, she has not truly left home.

Every couple needs to learn this lesson. You need to establish your home. You must make decisions based on what is best for your household, for you and your children.

I know that as I look at my children, especially as they approach the age to marry, I have to be willing to obey this Scripture and let them go. I continually read this verse to renew my heart and mind. I've put a lot into my children. I love them and love to be with them, but when they marry, I will have to obey the Word and even demand that they obey it.

If you're a parent who has not let go yet, do it now. Do it for your children and for your own marriage. This doesn't mean you cannot spend time with them. You can. But you need to build a godly relationship based on truth, and allow your children the freedom to establish their own home without feeling guilty if they don't do things the way you've always done them.

As I've reflected on our children someday getting married, I've considered Casey and me sitting down with each of them and their future mate and saying, "For so many years we have been our son's (or daughter's) parents. We love him, and we are sold out to him, but now you both are one, so you are both our children. Son (or daughter), your wife (or husband) is on equal footing now with us, so don't think we will take sides. Don't come to us to split you apart. You are joined together."

As I've thought about all of this, I've also realized that as parents, we cannot counsel our married children concerning their marriages. It's impossible not to take sides if your child runs back and forth between you and their spouse. Such children only tell Mom and Dad their side of the issues in their marriage. Then, when they go home and make it all right with their spouse, they don't go back and tell Mom and Dad how wrong they were. So Mom and Dad's opinion becomes skewed. Their opinion developed from what the child wanted them to hear out of hurt or anger.

Children, if you want your parents to love your mate, refuse to bring them into the issues or challenges of your marriage. You can still ask them for wisdom. There are all kinds of things young people should ask of those who have walked the road before them, but you have to guard yourself and your marriage.

The Word says "leave." Another way to say it is "depart." You are now joined to your mate. Your relationship with your parents must change. All of this affects your married relationship, and it will in some way affect your sex life.

A Gift With No Shame

Sex is God's gift to a husband and his wife with no shame attached to it. Genesis 2:25 says, "And they were both naked, the man and his wife, and were not ashamed." The shame of sex was introduced by sin when Adam and Eve fell in the Garden of Eden. (Gen. 3:6,7.) Shame comes from the world and the negativity around us.

When God made the man and his wife and brought them together, there was no shame. The fear, anxiety, pain, or failure we may experience concerning sex is the effect of Satan and sin in the world.

God created sex with the intent that when a husband or wife are naked with their spouse, they will never feel shame. If you feel ashamed, know that feeling isn't from God. He wants you to enjoy sex freely with your mate.

Many women have told me they hide under the covers during sex and don't watch. Some said they hide their bodies from their husbands. One women even told me proudly how she'd been married for fifty years, and her husband had never seen her naked.

Women like that often feel embarrassed. They feel shame. Many women have been taught sex is nasty, bad, ugly, and dirty. They are filled with guilt and condemnation. It's no wonder some couples have traumatic problems in their sex lives. They bring these thoughts into their marriage relationships.

Sometimes men are embarrassed too, although in general, they tend to be less modest about their bodies. Usually they don't care if all the curtains and windows are open, but women have a tendency to hide for such reasons as "Don't look at my hips. Don't look at how fat I am." But God says we should not be embarrassed.

If you think negatively about your body, then you will be uptight about your mate looking at, touching, or enjoying your body. Your mind will be on yourself instead of the joy in the gift God gave you.

I have known women who have been married fifteen or more years, who have never allowed their husbands to see them without their clothes on. They make their husbands turn out the lights so they won't see them. Some even avoid looking at their husbands as well. When you choose to behave like that, your mind shuts down, and your body responds accordingly. You cannot enjoy the celebration of love that God intended sex to be.

If you feel this way, God wants to help you renew your mind. Keep reading this book and by the end, you will be well on your way. Renew your mind to understand that when Adam and Eve were created, they came together, were naked, and were not ashamed. They did not look at each other and say, "I can't believe it. You are different than me," or "Wait a minute. Let me get some leaves."

They were never ashamed until sin entered the earth. When they ate from the tree of knowledge, sin entered the world, and they experienced shame. They hid from God (Gen. 3:8), but shame was never His plan for us.

Your body and your husband's body were created to be enjoyed by each other. His is yours, and yours is his. You are both God's creation. God has blessed each of you with the other to enjoy.

First Corinthians 7:1-4 says:

> Now concerning the things of which you wrote to me:
> It is good for a man not to touch a woman.

Nevertheless, because of sexual immorality, let each man have his own wife, and let each woman have her own husband.

Let the husband render to his wife the affection due her, and likewise also the wife to her husband.

The wife does not have authority over her own body, but the husband does. And likewise the husband does not have authority over his own body, but the wife does.

Sex within marriage is not sin. It is the most exciting gift on this earth. An open, free, and unashamed relationship with your spouse is normal.

If these words make you feel uncomfortable, then I hope that you will continue to read this book. God wants to help you. Regardless of what's holding you back, God can heal, transform, and set you free. Nothing is too big or hard for Him.

You may be haunted by your past. Maybe you were molested, raped, or had multiple sex partners before marriage. No matter what it is, God can heal you and set you free.

A good wife oversees her household. She makes sure everyone has clean clothes, the house is clean, everyone has a ride where they need to go, the dog gets to the vet, the groceries are bought and meals are planned, but she cannot leave out the priority of passion for her husband. If she does, the long-term consequences will catch up to her and prove painful.

God wants your marriage to thrive, and good sex is vital to your marriage. Good sex is enjoyable sex. Good sex is right and holy. Good sex is God's gift to you.

New Thoughts to Think

If barriers exist between you and your husband being naked in front of one another and not ashamed, ask God to reveal the source of the shame and to heal you and your husband. Begin to boldly declare, "I am made in the image and likeness of God, and my husband is made in the image and likeness of God. Therefore, I am not ashamed of how I look or uncomfortable to look at my husband, and I am able to enjoy sex with him."

2

Give Yourself Fully

The world is full of sex books, both good and not so good. Much of what I've read and been told in the world tells women, "In sex, get all you can and experience everything."

The message is to be selfish, and truthfully, I never thought about it until one day while meditating on the Word, I thought, *That principle goes against the Word because the Word never tells us to be selfish.*

God's message to us is "Give, and it will be given to you: good measure, pressed down, shaken together, and running over will be put into your bosom. For with the same measure that you use, it will be measured back to you." (Luke 6:38.)

As I read this Scripture in the context of a marital sexual relationship, I began to see a difference in what the world says and what God says. God's way is always better. I meditated even more, asking, *What does it mean, God, when all the sex therapists tell us to get, yet You are telling us to give?* And the answers began to come.

When we enjoy ourselves in the celebration of love to the very fullest, we give the greatest gift that we could ever give to our husbands. Something wonderful happens to a man when he has satisfied his wife sexually. Something happens to a woman when she gives herself fully to her man. Giving to each other does something emotionally that nothing else can do.

Obtaining sexual pleasure is a temporary, empty thrill, but giving to your mate in celebration of your love for each other brings a satisfaction that produces growth in your relationship like nothing else can.

Many women don't know how to give this way. They have a "duty" type of attitude toward sex. They think sex will keep their husband satisfied. They think, *It's no big deal* or that it's just something they're supposed to do because they are married. Many women believe they simply need to fulfill their husband's "needs" a certain number of times per month.

This is incorrect thinking. Women who want to do what they believe is their "duty" miss out on the plan of God for their marriage.

I love the story of Mary and Martha in the Bible. It illustrates the heart God wants us to have.

> Now it happened as they went that He entered a certain village; and a certain woman named Martha welcomed Him into her house.
>
> And she had a sister called Mary, who also sat at Jesus' feet and heard His word.
>
> But Martha was distracted with much serving, and she approached Him and said, "Lord, do You not care that my sister has left me to serve alone? Therefore tell her to help me."
>
> And Jesus answered and said to her, "Martha, Martha, you are worried and troubled about many things.
>
> "But one thing is needed, and Mary has chosen that good part, which will not be taken away from her."
>
> LUKE 10:38-42

Martha invited Jesus to come for dinner, but once He was there, and she was doing all the work required to make and serve dinner, she wanted to change her request. Mary probably didn't feel any obligation to help. This story suggests that she had not invited Him, so she did what she wanted—she listened to Jesus.

Martha in her predicament said to Jesus, "Make Mary work with me."

Jesus answered her, "Martha, Martha, you are worried and troubled about many things."

In the sexual relationship, many times we act like a Martha. We say yes, but we really want to say no. We have no Mary spirit at all. We say, "Yes, I'd like to have sex," but truthfully, it is a yes from the vocal chords and a no from the heart. To me, that demonstrates a Martha spirit.

Mary, on the other hand, said yes from the heart. She sat at Jesus' feet, and Jesus said, "...Mary has chosen that good part...." She had chosen to be true and honest. She was honest, not only in what she said, but also in her heart, from which she acted. They connected. She was saying the same thing in voice and action.

Many times women will say, "Yes, I enjoy sex," but on the inside they are screaming, "No!"

They communicate that no in many ways.

"Oh, don't look at me"—that's shame.

"I'm embarrassed about this"—that's shame.

"Don't touch me there"—that's fear.

In an intimate relationship, there must be vulnerability, openness, and a willingness to give to one another that says, "My arms belong to you. My fingers are yours. My neck is yours. My forehead is yours. My body is yours."

Our bodies don't really belong to us. As we saw earlier, "The wife does not have authority over her own body, but the husband does. And likewise the husband does not have authority over his own body, but the wife does" (1 Cor. 7:4).

Your body belongs to your husband, and his belongs to you. God said you do not have authority, or complete control, over your own body. It belongs to your mate.

The bottom line is, God wants a woman to give physical and sexual affection to her husband. Likewise, God wants a man to give the same to his wife.

I have a responsibility to give my body to Casey. It is a biblical, God-stated responsibility. I can't say, "I don't feel like it," because I don't have authority over my body. Neither can he say such a thing to me.

Everyone needs to forget the line about having a headache. Scriptures like 1 Corinthians 7:4 challenge us to face the areas where we need to change. They force us to ask ourselves, "Will I be a godly wife?" or "Will I be a godly husband? Am I going to do it my way or God's way?"

Remember, when you do it your way and the "warning light on the dash" comes on, then you're headed for trouble. Sure, the little light will eventually go off, but somewhere down the road you will come to a screeching halt, and it will probably be too late.

If, on the other hand, you go with God and allow Him to change you, then you'll experience fulfillment, health, and strength. You'll experience sex the way God intended for you.

You have to decide, "I'm going to change. I've been wrong. I did it the way my mama did it. I did it the way Daddy told me. I did it the way I saw on television, but I need to do it God's way."

Your attitude has to be, "This isn't just my body. This is my husband's (or wife's)." You have to give yourselves to each other as part of your Christian privilege.

Yes, sex is a desire. Yes, it's an exciting, fulfilling part of the marriage relationship that God put into your being. But it's also part of your spiritual, biblical responsibility.

Hear me correctly. This does not give either spouse the right to abuse. It does not give anyone the right to misuse or dominate another. It simply means it's your responsibility to give yourself sexually to your spouse.

The Joy of Frequency

Everyone always wants to know, "How often are we supposed to have sex?"

While most want to know how many times a week, when I teach seminars, I am sometimes asked, "How many times a day are normal for having sex? My husband wants it two, three, or four times a day."

After years of counseling couples, I personally believe that this is not a healthy way to live in a marriage relationship. In my experience, I have heard that several things happen when a person wants to have sex all the time. One, the husband probably isn't employed in a job he loves. Second, someone who wants to have sex that often may have something unfulfilled on the inside of him or her. They may have issues that need to be resolved. They may even have an addiction.

People can be addicted to sex the same as they can be addicted to drugs and alcohol. If your mate is addicted to sex, fight in the spiritual realm for him or her to be set free.[1] Pray and fast to break those bondages in his or her life. And if necessary, get great, mature Christian counseling. Your family and your marriage are worth an investment of prayer, fasting, and counseling. Freedom is worth it.

Hebrews 6:12 says that through faith and patience we inherit the promises of God. It takes time and spiritual fighting in certain areas of our lives to be free from bondages and addictions.

It's easier to not pray, not fast, and stay angry with your mate. It's easier to yell and scream, but that will never win him over. Praying and fasting, loving and giving, and knowing and applying what God's Word says will work.[2]

Please realize that I am sharing in general terms here. I want to emphasize that if there is any kind of abuse in your relationship, seek godly counsel. You need insight as well as healing.

For a good sense of what is normal for our marriages, 1 Corinthians 7:5,6 tells us:

> Do not deprive one another except with consent for a time, that you may give yourselves to fasting and prayer; and come together again so that Satan does not tempt you because of your lack of self-control.
>
> But I say this as a concession, not as a commandment.

We may not always feel like having sex, but if we want to give ourselves wholly to our mate, then we want to satisfy and please our partner. As mature Christians, we are not to live by our feelings.(2 Cor. 5:7.) We can't let a feeling of "I don't want to" stand in the way of giving.

Personally, I believe God set up our lives in a weekly pattern. The seven-day week in the Bible was a period of time during which certain things must happen. Weekly we worship and accomplish certain goals. Weekly we rest, revitalize, and recreate our beings. God's pattern of a seven-day cycle for our lives is obvious.

Even exercise has to be weekly. You may not exercise daily, but you need a good weekly plan where you work out two, three, or four days a week if you want to experience good results.

Casey and I have days when we are so busy that we don't even get to sit down and chat or really give attention to each other. We may grab ten minutes at the end of the day together, but because we are both very tired, it's off to sleep we go. If that were to continue for weeks, however, we would be in trouble. Our marriage would be affected.

You may miss certain things daily, but you can create a habit for your week. For example, you don't go to church every day, but you go a couple of times a week so your spiritual life stays strong. In the same way, a couple probably won't have sex every day, but they'd better integrate a regular sexual life into their week. The point is, it must be a regular part of your week. There's no law or rule on the amount of times each week. You don't say to your spouse, "Look, it's been three times this week, so back off." Or, "Hey, it's only been once this week, so you've got to get going."

No, you simply create a regular cycle where perhaps two, three, or four times a week you enjoy sex. I usually tell people that three times a week is a good rule of thumb.

This is not a law or a set number; it is just a suggestion. Have sex on a regular basis, and it ebbs and flows with what's going on in your life. Circumstances change throughout the seasons of our lives. Remember, in 1 Corinthians 7:5 Paul said that a key reason not to have sex was by mutual consent for fasting and praying.

Stoke the Fire

There are a lot of reasons why women don't enjoy sex, and I'm going to address many of those reasons in this book. For now, I want you to understand the gift that sex is, the beautiful act God made it to be, and how He intends for us to fully enjoy it. One of the ways to keep a fire going is to stoke it. A sure way to put it out is to douse it with cold water. In marriage, you have to stoke the fire year after year. In other words, you have to tend to the sexual relationship of your marriage.

I've watched some women who have been married for a number of years cease to give themselves wholly to their husbands. They douse the fire rather than stoke it. Gradually they begin to talk about their husbands and degrade them. They fail to appreciate their husbands and place demands on them. They sarcastically tell them exactly how they perceive them in every area of life.

This proves destructive to a man's ego. When a woman like that has sex with her husband, she has the Martha kind of attitude. She gives him sex, but she acts like a dead fish lying there. Her heart is not in it. She develops the attitude, "Sex is for him really, not me." If you feel that way, you're wrong. You're missing a great celebration that God has given you.

I've listened as women blamed their husbands for this and that. They've whined and said things such as, "Well, if he would just talk to me; if he would just share with me. If I could just share my heart with him."

While these may be legitimate desires, a woman like that is often what Proverbs equates to a dripping faucet: "A continual dripping on a very rainy day and a contentious woman are alike" (Proverbs 27:15). Or, as Proverbs 19:13 puts it, "...the contentions of a wife are a continual dripping."

A woman like this just "drips, drips, drips" year after year until she has built a wall. She finds fault with her husband because she's never truly appreciated who he is as a man. She's tried to make him something else, and she's never truly communicated with him. She must learn how to listen to him talk. She doesn't even know how to communicate her own emotions to him because she's used sarcasm, anger, bitterness, and manipulation to make him listen to her. She is not being honest with him.

Sometimes a woman actually tries to get her husband to act like a woman. She wants him to communicate with her in the same way as her girlfriends. He's not a woman; he's a man. He can't be your girlfriend. Refuse to become offended at every little thing he does because he doesn't act like your girlfriends.

Think about who your husband is. He's not the man in the romance novels you've read or the movies you've seen. Who is he, then? Find out who he is, and draw him to you. Entice him. Go after him. Appreciate him. Don't be a hard woman to live with. Proverbs 21:9 warns, "Better to dwell in a corner of a housetop, than in a house shared with a contentious woman."

I learned what I'm telling you years ago from a mistake I made with Casey. There was a very nice gentleman in our church at the time. He always ran ahead, opened the door for me, and offered to carry things for me. It got my attention, not in a sexual way, but I started to compare him to Casey.

Soon I started in on Casey, "Why can't you be like this person? Why can't you act like him? He always opens the door for me, and he's so kind." I compared and compared. I dripped and dripped. Six months later the man left our church. Seven months later he divorced his wife for his secretary.

The grass may look greener on the other side, but if you get close to the field, you'll see that it's only spray-painted green.

Eventually, I went to Casey and asked him to forgive me. I told him how much I liked who he was. Then I began to study Casey.

Who is my husband? Who is this man that attracted me to him?

I realized that when I met Casey, I had complete resolve that "He's it. I'm done with all the others. This is the man for me. I want him." What was it that did that to me?

The very thing that often attracts us to someone can become the very thing that bugs us the most later on. When I met Casey, I loved how serious-minded he was. That is what attracted me to him the most. It caused me to honor and respect him. Years later into our marriage I wanted to say, "Can't you be more fun?"

I had to stop myself and ask, "What am I looking for here? Why am I wanting to trade him in right now in my heart and mind?" You can't trade in your husband or try to mold him into a different man. If you do, your sexual relationship will go downhill.

What are you doing to serve your husband? What are you doing to give to him? What are you doing to strengthen him, to enhance his winning, conquering spirit—the spirit God put in all men?

Begin to see your husband as Tarzan. See him as the man God brought into the world as your conqueror.

Whatever you want, build it with your words. Proverbs 6:2 says, "You are snared by the words of your mouth; you are taken by the words of your mouth."

Be the "wise woman" in Proverbs 14:1 who "builds her house." Call those things that be not as though they were. (Rom. 4:17 KJV.)

New Thoughts to Think

Ask the Lord to show you how you can give yourself more fully to your husband. Begin to boldly declare, "I am a giver. I give freely and fully of myself to my husband, and it is returned to me good measure, pressed down, shaken together and running over. I thank You, Lord, that I am always honest in my heart and actions."

3

Fire Up Your Passion;
Extinguish Your Past

M arriage is covenant—the most powerful and passionate of relationships on earth established by
God Himself. Covenant is a relationship that cannot be
broken. When you have sex, you enter into covenant. You
become one with your spouse.

Popular teaching says you become soul mates, but there
is no such thing as a soul mate. When you have sex with
someone, you do not become one soul. It is not scriptural.
You become one flesh. That is God's description of the
husband and wife relationship. You enter into covenant.

When Adam sinned, the sin nature entered in, and
man was separated from God. Adam broke fellowship
with God, and God had to make a way for Adam to have

relationship with Him again. God's temporary answer was the laws of the Old Testament. The only atonement for sin was shed blood, the cut covenant.

In Genesis 3:21, God cut covenant with Adam and Eve. With the sacrifice of an animal and shed blood, which symbolized reconciliation, peace came between God and man.[1] Throughout the rest of the Old Testament, an animal was slain as the covenant between God and man for the forgiveness of sin.

Covenants were also cut between allies. If two leaders made a covenant and one leader and his people went to war, then the other leader and his people went to war with them. If one man didn't have money but was in covenant with someone, then the other man in covenant with him covered the debt. Whatever one person needed, the other person in covenant with him met the need.

Two people in covenant would die for each other. They were one. They were in covenant—just like marriage. In the Old Testament and throughout history, covenants were never intended to be broken.

Do you ever remember becoming "blood brothers" with a childhood friend? That was covenant. When the Indians cut their wrists and mingled blood, they cut covenant. They committed to die, if necessary, to protect one another. It is a lifetime bond that cannot be broken.

In the New Testament, our covenant with God is based on the shed blood of Jesus. He cut covenant with us by shedding His blood for our salvation. (Heb. 9:12-15.)

God even created the woman's body to bleed when she has sex for the first time. We will discuss this more later on, but it doesn't happen repeatedly. It is a one-time event that I believe signifies the making of a covenant between the man and the woman.

In our society today, integrity and honor have become optional, rather than the norm. There is no understanding of such absolutes as covenant. Evidence of that can be seen in the fact that divorce has become rampant. We lack true understanding of covenant.

If you are already married, keep in mind the importance of passing this knowledge of covenant on to your sons and daughters. If you are single, hide it in your heart.

The reason we are not to have sex outside of marriage is that it is an act of covenant. We become one with the person with whom we have sex.

Now, if you had sex before marriage or were promiscuous, don't give in to condemnation. I have encouraging news for you in the following pages. God wants you to extinguish the past and learn how to fire up your future.

If I asked everyone in the groups to which I minister to raise their hands if they were not a virgin on their wedding night, probably the majority of women would acknowledge they had sex before marriage. Regardless of our own personal experiences, we have to know the truth God established before we were ever born.

Remember, sex is the most unique and beautiful gift that anyone can give his or her spouse. God established this covenant; therefore, it's important that we don't cut it with just anyone. The sexual relationship, as planned by God, is not a one-night stand or passing pleasure. It is a covenant we cling to as we give ourselves wholly to the person with whom we have chosen to live our lives in marriage. This covenant is a lifetime commitment.

From Wounds to Scars

Gift or no gift, many women don't enjoy sex. They would love to give themselves wholly to their husbands, but frankly, they feel locked into the emotions that flood their souls.

They would love to have things differently in their marriage, and perhaps they have in spurts, but overall they feel hopeless and powerless to change.

For change to come, healing and forgiveness must come first. The wounds must heal, and a time of recovery is necessary.

I experienced this physically when I was eleven years old. A car hit me. It was a traumatic event, and I was seriously injured. I was first hurled through the air, and then I slid on the ground. Blood was everywhere. It was a terrible sight.

Through the ordeal of initially being treated, transported to the hospital, and put back together, my family and friends all thought, *She's going to die. It's so horrible. She won't make it.*

My recovery took weeks, but I healed physically and emotionally. Today I have a huge scar on my left leg and scars on my toes and forehead. I described all of that just enough to give you a picture.

When you are hit emotionally, no matter how it occurs, God can heal you. Yes, in the beginning you may be laid wide open and in horrible pain. Some people go through emotional injuries that are more dramatic, ugly, and hurtful than others, but God can still heal them.

You may be left with a scar. I was left with one on my leg, but I rarely think about it. It doesn't hurt, and it doesn't affect me. I don't go through emotional turmoil when I think about the fact that I was hit by a car, flew through the air, and slid on the ground. I'm not afraid to ride in a car, drive a car, or cross a street filled with traffic.

I am healed—spirit, soul, and body. You can be too.

If you have sexual scars in your past that cause you shame or hurt, God can heal them. Maybe you were raped. Maybe it was incest with a brother, sister, father, or stepfather who violated you.

Regardless of your past injury, you can choose to be healed, or you can live the rest of your life wrapped in the chains that have kept you bound thus far.

You have to make a decision. Ask yourself, "What am I going to do? Am I going to feel bad forever because I was foolish enough to have sex with every guy who wanted to?"

Maybe you had no moral training. Maybe your parents never taught you concerning your sexuality. Then again, maybe you had everything you needed to make the right choices, but you simply chose to break the rules.

You can go on in your current state of hurt, or you can be healed and live free the rest of your life. Just admit that it happened and ask for forgiveness; then you can move forward. First John 1:9 says that if you ask God to forgive you, He will cleanse you from all unrighteousness.

Whether it's sexual affairs or pornography, deal with it. Get help to cut it off. God wants you to be free to enjoy sex with your spouse. When you have issues haunting you, you cannot enjoy sexual intimacy, and you are incapable of giving yourself wholly to your mate, much less receiving wholly from him.

You can't truly be "...naked...and...not ashamed."

In Hebrews 13:4 AMP God Himself tells us, "Let marriage be held in honor...And...the marriage bed...undefiled (kept undishonored)...." So don't take the baggage of shame from incidents in your past to bed with you.

Talk to that baggage. Tell it, "I'm not going to carry you around with me anymore. You don't belong in my heart and mind anymore." If someone violated you, you may need to do something visual to mark the time you made the choice to forgive the person, whether it is the person who knew what was happening but didn't come to your defense or yourself for choices you made. Then you need to ask God to forgive you and receive His forgiveness.

In some cases I also suggest that people write down past wounds on a sheet of paper, and place the paper in a box. Then take it outside, talk to God, and set it on fire. Have a "God celebration" and speak to the past, "You're gone. It's gone—and I'm free from that in the name of Jesus. I'm not going to be bound to what happened in the past.

That's not who I am now. The Bible says I am a new creature in Christ Jesus." (2 Cor. 5:17.) Get rid of it—spiritually, emotionally, and physically.

You have to deal with the unforgiveness, the bitterness, and any negative thoughts about past sexual relationships that you have brought into your marriage. Sex is not dirty or bad. It may feel dirty or bad to you, but God wants to heal you of that. It is difficult to overcome these kinds of feelings, so we must have help.

The only way people can be totally free is through the power and love of the Holy Spirit working in them, helping them to forgive and overcome. For those who don't know Jesus as their Lord and Savior, it is much more difficult and devastating to overcome.

Too often a woman who has experienced some kind of sexual perversion in the past thinks, *I'm the only one this happened to.* She feels guilty, bad, or evil. If that is you, know that you are not alone, and you don't have to feel guilty for the rest of your life. You don't have to hold on to the bitterness and the hurt.

The negative past affects your present perspective of sex. It usually has nothing to do with your mate. No matter how many years you've been married, if you've brought your past along with you, you have skewed your sexual relationship. It has been darkened and carries the weight of your past. Guilt comes with it.

Guilt can be easily recognized.

"I shouldn't do this. I shouldn't enjoy this. I shouldn't be doing this."

All the "shouldn'ts" are the lack of freedom that has caused you to shut down emotionally—and when you shut down emotionally, you shut down physically as well.

God wants you to enjoy the freedom, the inside vulnerability, the inside abandonment to your husband, to who he is as a man. God wants to touch that part of your heart and make it come alive. All you have to do is ask Him to do it.

Now, if you have shut down, your husband has probably shut down as well. Many men shut down hope without knowing what they are doing. They shut down emotionally and live that way so long that they don't know what they may have been hoping for. They don't know what they could have.

But when you get free, and you stoke his fire, he may be confused at first: "We've been this way for ten years. What's wrong with the way things are?"

He's gotten into a routine of who you are, but now you've changed. So don't back off. Let the fire burn. Stoke it. Soon you'll see him come alive. His hopes will be sparked, and you will both have what God always intended for you to enjoy.

Leave Your "Exes" Behind

If a husband or wife has been married before, the memory of that previous spouse needs to be healed and released. For example, if your first husband abused you, used you, and left you, and you've never let God heal you, you may walk around now in your current marriage guarding yourself and protecting yourself. You may have walls up in preparation for your present husband to do the same thing. The truth is, by not being healed, you're actually setting him up to do the same thing.

You have to forget what is behind. You have to forget that first marriage. You can't compare. Don't ever bring up comparisons. Don't talk about it to your present spouse. As far as your spouse is concerned, you should speak and act as though you never had a first husband or wife or even a girlfriend or boyfriend. You should act as though you've never even noticed another woman or man on earth. Husbands, as far as your wife is concerned, you can't even remember another female's name. You've forgotten there were other women around. Wives, the same is true for you about other men. That has to be your attitude toward things of the past.

Sex Before Marriage

Another thief in marriage comes on the scene if you've had premarital sex, especially if it was with the man who is now your husband. Women often hold this against themselves and their spouse. To bury it, they say, "It's okay."

If that describes you, understand that the worst thing you can ever do for your soul (your mind, will, and emotions) is to "OK" something that isn't okay. That's denial. It was sin. It was wrong, and you knew it. But let 1 John 1:9,10 encourage you: "If we confess our sins, He is faithful and just to forgive us our sins and to cleanse us from all unrighteousness. If we say that we have not sinned, we make Him a liar, and His word is not in us."

So you've carried this sin and been mad at yourself and at him. And it has affected your intimacy. You hold on to little things inside you that feel like giant brick walls you can't scale. The walls hold you back from the intimacy you desire.

Husbands and wives have to cleanse their hearts. I've not met one woman who had sex before marriage who was not ashamed of it. And when a man doesn't deal with the shame, his wife carries it.

Men don't seem to bring any of the baggage I described earlier into marriage, but women do. Nonetheless, men have the responsibility of cleaning up the shame.

A man needs to talk to his wife and make it right, especially if he was her one and only. She feels like she ruined it. The truth is, you both ruined it. And you didn't lead well. You didn't honor her. You didn't respect her enough to guard the most precious gift that a person can give to another. You didn't love her enough to wait. It's a one-time gift, and you took it without a covenant of marriage, and you left emptiness in its place. You left a lack of fulfillment.

No matter how many years you've been married, you both need to go back and clean it up. Go back to the beginning, and go through the issues. Even if you weren't saved, it's still sin. Just ask for forgiveness, and move forward.

You can have something better. God wants you to be the most vulnerable and most open with this person. You're naked with this person physically, so be naked in your emotions too. Risk it. Step out and start the process for something different than what you've had.

If you have secrets, things you've kept from one another, clean that up too. You don't have to go into great detail, but get the facts out into the open.

For example, you could say "Honey, I just wanted you to know that I had sex before we were married." Get it out into the open. Keep no secrets.

God's forgiveness is big enough for whatever you have to confess. His forgiveness is big enough to forgive anyone's past.

When I called my Mom more than twenty years ago and told her I was marrying Casey and that he was in a drug rehabilitation program, you can imagine what went through her mind. But God's forgiveness was big enough for Casey. My Mom had prayed for my mate and all of my brothers' and sisters' mates all our lives. In the end we all married very well, but not all of our spouses came from picture-perfect backgrounds.

Whatever your past story is, it is time for you to allow the healing virtue of the Lord Jesus Christ to remove every blockage that keeps you from totally abandoning yourself to your husband. You can allow the Holy Spirit to take His thread of love, mercy, and healing power and stitch up your wounds. You can walk through the healing and recovery phase. You may come out with a few scars and dents, but they won't hurt. You'll know they are there, but they'll never hold you back again.

The Myth of Good Girls vs. Bad Girls

Our society has double standards. For example, years ago as Casey and I were discussing this, I said, "I hear a lot of preachers who talk about girls being virgins. Excuse me. Is there something in the Bible that talks about a guy not having to be a virgin when he marries?"

Casey had a truthful observation: "The responsibility of the sexual "no" has been put upon the women of society. If you want to be a good girl, you are the one who says no. Of course, there are always some 'bad' girls out there. So the guys say, 'Oh, yeah, those are the ones you date, and the good girls are the ones you marry.'" You've probably heard these kinds of comments before.

Both men and women have so many mixed signals and messages. In order to prove their manliness, men are supposed to be sexually active. Women have to prove their womanliness by staying pure. This is unfair. Men have had pressure placed on them to be "real men" by proving their sexuality. They are expected to "get some." But "real women" are to "get none." Both ideas have led to a very wrong way of thinking in the sexual relationship. As a result, many women walk into marriage believing bad girls "do it," good girls don't. It can take years to get through a concept that has been planted into so many of us.

I teach my daughter and sons that it's not a matter of bad or good. It's a matter of "It's a wonderful God-plan when you are married. Sex is a gift from God that He has given you for marriage. Having sex before you are married will never bring peace or joy. It will never bring you fulfillment in your heart."

Of course, sex can give pleasure in a purely physical sense, and I tell my kids that. I don't lie to them. But I teach them God's truth about it.

I explain to my children that sex before marriage will eat you up inside, because God has written in your heart the right thing to do. If you go against His plan, it just hurts you. It is painful and ugly.

I have always taught my children to feel badly when they do anything against the Word. I put words to that feeling inside of them. I want them to know it feels bad when they lie or go against the truths of God's Word in any way.

As 2 Corinthians 7:10,11 teaches us, godly sorrow leads to repentance. Our children need to know and understand it.

I remember one Sunday morning as I walked through Casey's office at the church, one of our children jumped up and came running out with that fearful look seven-year-olds can have when they've been caught doing something wrong. He had been watching television when he should have been in church.

I asked him, "You were doing something wrong, weren't you?"

After he acknowledged his sin, we talked. I said, "That feels horrible, doesn't it, son? You never want to have that horrible, bad, yucky feeling of lying to Mommy and Daddy again. Let's pray and ask God to forgive you."

He asked God to forgive him, and he asked Casey and I to forgive him.

Then I said, "Now, doesn't that feel good?"

"Yeah," he smiled.

"That's walking clean and happy inside," I explained.

God wants the husband and wife to walk clean and happy before each other. He wants the husband and the wife to enjoy the sexual relationship.

It's Not the Past—It's the Present

Sometimes the past has nothing to do with why women don't like sex. Their husbands and the present can rob them of the joy of sex.

Proverbs 5 admonishes husbands:

> Drink water from your own cistern, and running water from your own well.
>
> Should your fountains be dispersed abroad, streams of water in the streets?
>
> Let them be only your own, and not for strangers with you.

Let your fountain be blessed, and rejoice with the wife of your youth.

As a loving deer and a graceful doe, let her breasts satisfy you at all times; and always be enraptured with her love.

PROVERBS 5:15-19

Husbands, your attention is to be in one place and one place only—in "your own cistern." It's not in sexually explicit magazines or movies or on the Internet. You are not to allow yourself to be sexually entertained anywhere else but in "your own cistern."

Magazines, movies, and sex-related Internet Web sites don't help you have great sex. They simply distract you and hurt your wife.

You may say, "Oh, but my wife enjoys it because we watch movies together." If that's true, she has become darkened in her heart. She has been put down, and her low self-image has allowed these things to come into her life. This is also characteristic of a woman who allows herself to be beaten and abused.

Allowing things such as pornography into the home is a sign of weakness in both the man and the woman. A man who brings pornography into his home is flesh-minded instead of spirit-minded.

Don't be deceived into thinking regular television is not pornographic. Many times it is simply cheap pornography. Realize certain kinds of TV shows can lure your mind to go in the wrong direction. It lures you into thinking of other "cisterns," other women, to "drink" from. It promotes fantasies about other women.

Ephesians 5:25 tells men, "Husbands, love your wives, just as Christ also loved the church and gave Himself for her." It is repulsive to think of Christ violating His love for the church so cheaply by giving in to doing something so vile. He loves us. He guards us. That's why He gave His life for us.

Husbands, recognize that Jesus' level of calling and commitment is the same as yours. It is a call God has placed on you for your wife. If you deny that call, you allow the devil to rip you off with his lies. He can trick you if he gets you to put your job, sports, pornography, or anything else ahead of your wife. He has deceived you to keep you from truly knowing all you could really have.

I realize many people were not raised in healthy homes. So it's hard for some to picture what I'm describing. Nonetheless, it is worth going after. As a couple, it may take you a month, a year, or five years to get there—but it's well worth it.

Let your fountain be blessed, and rejoice with the wife of your youth.

As a loving deer and a graceful doe, let her breasts satisfy you at all times; and always be enraptured with her love.

PROVERBS 5:18,19

New Thoughts to Think

If you had premarital sex with your mate or someone else, forgive and release that person. Repent of any pent-up anger, hurt, and bitterness. Ask the Holy Spirit to replace the negative attributes with joy. Then thank the Lord for giving you "beauty for ashes, the oil of joy for mourning," and "the garment of praise for the spirit of heaviness." (Isa. 61:3.) Rejoice in the newfound freedom that follows.

4

Great Sex Doesn't Come Naturally

I am amazed at all the ways women devise to keep from going to bed at the same time as their husbands. Women have told me they go to bed a little bit earlier, stay up and watch a late show, take a lot longer to floss their teeth, brush their teeth, wash their face, and on and on the list goes—as well as telling me the other problems in their marriage.

There are women who wear three gowns tied up to their chins, all in an effort to truly turn their husband off. Then there are always the excuses, "I'm really tired tonight. I just can't seem to get rid of this headache."

Their signals are loud and clear: "Don't touch me!"

As mentioned earlier, women who practice diversion tactics think of sex as a duty. They believe it is something they must do because they are married. They feel that the sooner each sex act is over, the better. When it's over, they think they have done their duty for the week or month. They have such a negative concept about the sexual part of their married relationship.

If you are one of those women, I believe the reason you think of sex as a duty is that you've never really enjoyed it. You've never experienced a real climax. You've never enjoyed the fulfillment that God wants every married person to have.

When a woman does not reach a climax on a regular basis, she misses God's plan for her sexual relationship with her husband. When that happens, it's no small wonder that sex becomes a duty instead of pleasure.

Many women don't even know they've never experienced a climax. It's actually easy to have sex and never climax. If you have ever come to a climax, you know it. There is absolutely nothing else like it in your life. There is nothing that compares or relates to it.

Some women are tormented by this fact. They have a guilt complex and think such things as, *I wonder if there is something wrong with me. I wonder if I'm doing everything I should. Is there something wrong with my body? Is there something wrong with the way my husband is?*

All of these concerns bring torment, and most couples never talk about it.

Well, ladies, I'm going to talk about it. God wants your sex life to be earthshaking—not just okay.

Women have the image that men get to do everything, and we get the bottom of the barrel. That is not the way God set it up. God created us both for good sex. God didn't say, "Well, man, take advantage of the woman and have a good time." That's the image many women have had. We haven't recognized that God wants us to have the very best in every area of our lives—including a wonderfully satisfying sexual relationship with our husband.

Have you ever noticed how every time people have sex on television the first time everything turns out perfectly, and everything seems to be just wonderful? Television shows us how people just "jump in the sack," have sex, and every time it's a wonderful experience. Well, television leaves out a lot of truth and reality.

For example, men don't know what to do just because they are men. There is nothing innately inborn that causes a person to know how to perfectly please their mate. Men and women have to learn how to have good sex with their spouse, and it takes time.

Often women have placed high expectations on their husbands because "The guys in the movies always know what to do." The world has portrayed men as the ones who know everything about sex. But where did they learn it all? If they haven't had sex with you, then they don't know anything about sex with you.

You are supposed to teach your husband about having sex with you. The two of you are supposed to teach each other. You are supposed to learn about each other—to experiment, experience, and explore the sexual relationship together.

First-time experiences are not always exciting for a woman. A wedding night may not be all fireworks for a woman who is a virgin. It can be painful because of the tightness of her vagina. There can be a little pain or a lot. A piece of skin called a hymen[1] breaks the first time a woman is penetrated, and there can be a small amount of bleeding.

Men aren't usually taught this, and women don't typically climax where there's pain. Men need to go extremely slow on the wedding night. When men learn to go slow— early in marriage and years later too—their wives can come to a climax.

Reaching a climax doesn't come naturally. That's because great sex does not come naturally. You have to work at it and practice it. You have to learn how to have great sex.

With that said, I want to give you some tips on things you can do to help yourself reach a climax and how you can give yourself more fully to your mate so that you enjoy sex.

The following is a list of hindrances that could be keeping you from a climax. Read them and consider your marriage relationship. If not dealt with properly, they can hold you back.

1. POOR COMMUNICATION

In his book *Sex Begins in the Kitchen,* Dr. Kevin Leman describes communication as the "'sharing of yourself verbally and nonverbally in such a way as to enable someone else to understand what you've said and how you feel.' Communication involves not only the sharing of words, but just as importantly, the skills of listening and understanding."[2]

Clear communication deals with the issues before bed. You can never fully enjoy a sexual relationship with your mate if you have unforgiveness or bitterness in your heart. The sexual relationship is a celebration of love, and when you have bitterness or other negative emotions, you have a blockage that will show up in your sexual relationship. You cheat yourselves when you don't deal with those issues.

2. THE PAST

I have already devoted an entire chapter to this, but it is critical to your present sex life.

Things from your past that you've not overcome may not have anything to do with your husband. If you have past hurts, wounds, and bad experiences and have never been cleansed and healed of them, you take them to bed every time—even things you really had no control over. Many people have never shared some of the things that have happened in their past and been freed from them. They are still holding on because they think it was their fault, which is a perversion. For example, someone who was molested by their father may think, *I must have done something wrong for that to happen to me. How come I told my Mom, and she never made my Dad stop?*

There may be a lot of bitterness and unforgiveness that needs to be resolved in your inner person, and it has nothing to do with your husband. If so, until you are healed from those past experiences, sex will remain dirty, bad, or hurtful to you.

James 5:16 says, "Confess your trespasses to one another, and pray for one another, that you may be healed...."

You may not want to reveal the hurtful parts of your life, but continuing to keep them to yourself stops the healing power of God from coming into your situation and healing you.

3. FANTASIES

Many times women have fantasies in their minds from perversion they've seen on television so they cannot have a real relationship. If you have perverted yourself sexually by watching a lot of soap operas, bad movies, or reading lustful romance novels, then your thinking and your body are affected. The biggest sex organ you have is above your neck. It's your mind. If you have filled your mind with distorted images, you have wrongly affected your sexual relationship with your spouse. Books, movies, and television do not paint a picture of reality.

4. APATHY

Apathetic people basically don't want to do anything. They don't really care about doing anything to improve their sexual relationship and ability to come to a climax. They have an attitude that everything is fine the way it is, and they don't want to "work on it."

5. FEAR

The Bible teaches us that when we're married, we're not to be embarrassed or ashamed to look at each other's bodies, that we are to be free with each other as husband and wife. But too many people are inhibited in their body. They want to hide from their mate. When you want to hide yourself, you are never free with your mate—at least not as free as God desires you to be.

6. BEING OVERWEIGHT

Weight often does have something to do with a satisfying sex life. I bring this out because if you are overweight, then it may cause you to be uptight about your body. You may think about it. You may be flesh-conscious and inhibited in the sense of letting your mate look at you and touch you. It is important that our bodies be in good physical shape so we can enjoy all the things God has for us. I'm not saying that you have to be five feet seven inches tall and weigh 100 pounds. That would be ridiculous. I do mean that you should be comfortable with your own body. You should feel good about yourself and not be uptight, thus allowing yourself to be free in your body with your mate. With God's help, you can be. (Zech. 4:6; Phil. 2:13 AMP; Heb. 4:16.)

7. MASTURBATION

Another thing that can stop you from enjoying a fulfilling sexual relationship with your husband or wife is masturbation. If you practice masturbation, it may cause you to feel that you don't need a spouse or that a spouse can never fulfill you like you think you can fulfill yourself. I believe you have perverted your own body so that you cannot enjoy sex with your spouse.

Opinions vary regarding masturbation. While some engage in it without any sense of shame, guilt, or impropriety, others feel it is wrong. Actually, the Word of God has nothing to say to encourage it. The Word never tells you to be involved in making yourself come to a climax. It does tell you that you are to work with your spouse as a team—to cling to, to rely on, to be a part of one another as one flesh.

First Corinthians 7:1-5 is a healthy reminder:

> Now concerning the things of which you wrote to me: It is good for a man not to touch a woman.
>
> Nevertheless, because of sexual immorality, let each man have his own wife, and let each woman have her own husband.
>
> Let the husband render to his wife the affection due her, and likewise also the wife to her husband.
>
> The wife does not have authority over her own body, but the husband does. And likewise the husband does not have authority over his own body, but the wife does.
>
> Do not deprive one another except with consent for a time, that you may give yourselves to fasting and prayer; and come together again so that Satan does not tempt you because of your lack of self-control.

Although I am primarily addressing married relationships, I have included a chapter written specifically for singles and the issues they face. I know many singles will read this book, so I would be remiss if I didn't give them straightforward information to help them prepare for marriage. I love to study and talk with people about what brings success—and failure—in relationships. Therefore, and especially since I am discussing the detriments of masturbation, I would be remiss if I didn't expose what I believe is the destruction that masturbation causes in the life of a single person.

Through the years of listening and learning, I have discovered that many times we set ourselves up to fail. By "fail" I mean we don't have true success in the areas that are vital to living in the way God intended for us to live.

So, single reader, I have to consider the possibility of masturbation in your life as well—and I want to warn you of failure. If you masturbate you may very well be sabotaging your future marriage relationship, because for one thing it may seriously lessen your desire for a mate. God loves us tremendously, and He wants the best for us in every area of our lives, even our sex life. He put the desire for a sexual union in each one of us. It is a driving force that propels us toward a marriage relationship. When you take that desire and don't allow it to motivate you positively to pursue God's gift of a mate, then you aren't experiencing God's best for you, and you destroy His plan for your life.

I feel very strongly that if you masturbate, whether single or married, you should go before God and repent. Allow

His Holy Spirit to cleanse you, heal you, and create a new heart for your future. Then make the decision to move forward. If you are single, move forward, believing God to meet your need and bring that godly mate into your life.

8. YOUR TIME SCHEDULE

You can literally get so busy that you don't give any time to develop a good relationship with your mate. You go to bed and barely get enough sleep for the next day. If that is true, who wants to spend time having sex? You just want to sleep. Why is your time schedule so tight that you can never give of yourself to your mate? If that's the case, then it's time to make some changes.

Build True Intimacy
Through Communication

Think about it. When you enjoy sex, how does your husband respond? He's happy, isn't he? It fulfills him to see you satisfied, because he wants you to enjoy it just as much as he does. It is the most meaningful to your mate when you enjoy sex to the fullest.

On a scale from one to ten, we need to get up to the eights, nines, and tens on a consistent basis. We need to reach a climax consistently, and one of the ways we can do this is through honest communication.

Communicating openly with your mate so he knows what you like is not a selfish act. It may seem like you are selfishly asking him to meet your needs and that you are putting a demand upon him. That is very far from the truth. In reality, the more you communicate the better your sexual relationship will be and the more each of you will enjoy it.

Remember, selfishness tries to get. It is a negative action. Communication will bring about a true intimacy and vulnerability in your relationship. Our motivation should be to give of ourselves so wholly to our husband that we want him to better understand our needs physically, so we give him insight into what we like.

We need to talk to our spouses so they understand what is happening in our bodies. Men don't understand a woman's body unless it is explained to them. Women seem to expect a man to understand everything going on in a woman's body, but that's not realistic.

We've watched too many movies where the men seem to know everything that's going on, so we think, *Why doesn't my husband know?* Those guys depicted on television don't know anything. The characters they portray are simply involved in lust and sin—plus, the director tells the actors what to do.

As a wife it's your job to help your husband by showing him, talking to him, and helping him do what you need to be fulfilled, especially as your body changes.

Our bodies go through monthly cycles, and our desires change accordingly. Pregnancy, nursing, aging, and menopause change our bodies so that one week we might say "Do this," and the next week we may say "I don't want that." The bottom line is, what works one week doesn't necessarily work the next because of change. So we have to communicate to our spouse.

Another great idea is to read books. There is nothing wrong with obtaining information to help you grow in your marriage relationship, because frankly, you don't know everything. One of my all-time favorites is Tim and Beverly LaHaye's classic, *The Act of Marriage*.[3] I encourage you to buy the book and check into a hotel with your spouse for the weekend. Say, "Honey, we need to practice." Just read and practice, read and practice.

Here's another idea you can try at home. Turn off the television early one night. Check on your kids to ease your mind that they are all right. Then lock your bedroom door. You can't always wait until your kids are all in bed to be intimate with your spouse. If your kids are old enough to be on their own, try to forget about them for a little while. Put the CD player by the door. If the kids ask, "Why do you have a CD player on?" Say, "We want to. Please don't ask again." That's all you have to say. Then read and practice, read and practice. Just try it.

One more suggestion: If the kids aren't home, and you're going to have sex somewhere else in the house, remember to close the blinds.

I've said it before, and I'll say it again: A good sexual relationship with your mate doesn't come naturally.

There are certain things in our lives that we learn naturally, and there are certain things that just happen naturally. Your hair and fingernails grow naturally, but good sex doesn't. That is probably one of the greatest misconceptions in married life. People believe that things are just supposed to work naturally. They think, *Just get going, and it will all fall into place.*

Wrong. It's time to get some books.

I read books on how to train my children, how to cook, how to walk in faith and in the power of the Holy Spirit, how to be prosperous, and how to walk in joy. I also read my Bible all the time. Why not read a good book on how to have better sex?

Many good books can give us insight and wisdom on how to get things together and enjoy this wonderful gift God has given us.

Don't let embarrassment hold you back. I remember recommending to one woman that she buy a particular book I had read. She went to the bookstore and thumbed through it. When she saw the pictures of sex organs, she put it down and was too embarrassed to buy it. She later told me, "I couldn't buy that book. I was so embarrassed for anyone to know I was buying it."

Well, it's true; they would know it. If you think about it, people know when you buy other things too—like the things you buy at the drugstore. But it's all part of the facts of life. It's time to get over embarrassment, because we should not live embarrassed over a gift God has given to us.

What's the difference in buying a book on knowing the gifts of the Spirit or one on knowing what my body is to do in the sexual relationship? One of the books is easy to buy because it is spiritual. "Yes, I'm going to know about the gifts of the Spirit. Praise the Lord." We show off the book. It's like giving fifty dollars in the offering. We want to make sure people know it's not one dollar. We show it off a little bit.

Yet we purchase a book on sex and hide it under our coat, hoping no one announces it over the loud speaker. We shouldn't have this kind of attitude. Some people think, *If I buy a book, it's admitting I have a problem.* No, it means you want to learn. You want to have knowledge about the things you don't know. You want information and to change your way of thinking.

When you buy a sex book, you are not saying, "We have problems." You are saying, "I want the absolute best possible sexual relationship with my husband."

A good, powerful, wonderful sexual relationship does not happen by accident. It happens through continual wisdom and understanding. The Word says we are destroyed for a lack of knowledge. (Hosea 4:6.) God wants us to continue in our understanding and in our knowledge of gaining the most wonderful sexual relationship that He has ordained for us to have.

God wants you to love sex. Don't miss it anymore. Learn to communicate. Learn to climax. Learn how to have great sex.

New Thoughts to Think

Ask the Lord to help you live Ephesians 4:32 AMP daily in your relationship with your mate: "Become useful and helpful and kind to one another, tenderhearted (compassionate, understanding, loving-hearted), forgiving one another [readily and freely], as God in Christ forgave you." This type of heart attitude in you toward your mate will enhance your ability to give yourself wholly to him (or her).

5

What Sex Means to a Woman and a Man

Watching TV talk shows, comedies, movies, and reading the cover headlines of many women's magazines, one major focus seems to be communicated: Women do not enjoy sex. Or the focus is that sex is either no big deal, or you have to know all the newest "tricks" in order to satisfy your man. The media seems to communicate regularly that we have some sort of a problem. If you listen to some of the jokes and comments women make about men, you will often hear how they feel about their sex life.

Interestingly, I don't think it's because men have not cared or have not taken the time or have not been patient or kind. I think they just don't understand what sex means to a woman.

Sex fulfills a wife's womanhood and her self-esteem. When a woman has a horrible sexual experience and things just don't work out right in the sexual relationship, she feels bad inside. She lacks fulfillment. I've been told stories of how women cry themselves to sleep after unfulfilled sex. Too often couples complete the sex act, and the husband goes to sleep while the wife rolls over and cries for hours.

God's plan for the sexual relationship is to build up the woman, not pull her down. Most women remember when their sex life was "hot city." Everything was wonderful. So it hurts when the sexual relationship becomes unfulfilling.

Sex reassures a woman of her husband's love for her. I realize it can do the opposite in some marriages. If your husband isn't caring, it can reinforce feelings that he doesn't care, even though it may be that he is simply ignorant of how to express his love for you. Sex satisfies a woman's sex drive. "Oh, but Wendy, I don't have a sex drive."

If you are a woman, you do. Don't tell me if your husband were gone for three months, you wouldn't have some kind of desire. Some women are never apart from their husbands for any length of time to discover that they really do have that sexual desire.

Remember the first time you kissed? Remember the excitement you felt for each other? It's still inside you. God put that desire there. Now, it might have dried up through bitterness and unforgiveness, through hurt and disappointments, but it's still in you, and sex satisfies that desire.

Sex reduces friction in the home and nervousness within a woman. It relaxes the entire nervous system. After you have good sex, you are relaxed. The house could fall down, and your response would be, "Honey, maybe we should think about getting out of here." The nervousness of life diminishes.

Think about all of the stress in your life. Rather than have sex and eliminate much of it, women have a tendency to say to their husbands, "Honey, I don't have time right now because I have to do this, and this, and this."

They're so frazzled, they don't even realize that sex will benefit them greatly.

The sexual relationship provides heaven on earth. It is the best thing on earth that you can experience. If you don't feel that way, then you haven't experienced all that God planned for you as a woman. Read those books I mentioned earlier. Find out how this organ works and how that organ functions. I'm not going into those details, because my passion is to help you with the attitude of your mind toward sex. And God wants wives to enjoy it.

One of the couples in our church told me that they took a book and went away on a weekend retreat—just like I've recommended to you. They read the book and figured out how to do everything described in it. The wife said it was the first time she had ever experienced an orgasm. It wasn't that her husband didn't love her or that anything was wrong with her or even that they didn't diligently try to learn the right things to do. They simply had never had all the information and practice they needed to succeed.

Remember, good sex doesn't happen by accident. Whether you've been married five years or fifty years, between you and God, you will figure this out. He didn't mistakenly fashion a man and a woman to fit together. Now there's an amazing thought.

Think of the creativity, as well as what was in the heart of God, when it came to fitting a man and woman together. It is a miracle. Think about the physical body of the woman, the physical body of the man, and how God knew what would please a woman and what would please a man. Then He said, "Be one." It was His plan. Don't be embarrassed to say, "God, help me understand Your way."

You may be thinking, *I don't feel my sexual relationship is like heaven on earth. It doesn't relax me. I get angry, and it doesn't fulfill my womanhood. I simply don't like it.*

You can assist your husband in understanding you. Teach him what pleases you. Some women want a different kind of stimulus than what their husband knows to give them. Love is love, but there are different avenues in which it is expressed and communicated.

A Deep Well

Some men simply don't understand how a man is a fountain and a woman is a well. Proverbs 5:15-23, which I've quoted before, is very insightful:

Drink water from your own cistern, and running water from your own well.

Should your fountains be dispersed abroad, streams of water in the streets?

Let them be only your own, and not for strangers with you.

Let your fountain be blessed, and rejoice with the wife of your youth.

As a loving deer and a graceful doe, let her breasts satisfy you at all times; and always be enraptured with her love.

For why should you, my son, be enraptured by an immoral woman, and be embraced in the arms of a seductress?

For the ways of man are before the eyes of the LORD, and He ponders all his paths.

His own iniquities entrap the wicked man, and he is caught in the cords of his sin.

He shall die for lack of instruction, and in the greatness of his folly he shall go astray.

Husband, your wife is a well, and a well is deep. Before there were modern tools and equipment, families had to go out to the well and lower a rope that was tied to the bucket until the bucket hit water. Once it was full, they had to slowly pull the rope back up. It took time. They couldn't just turn on the faucet like we do today. They had to reach down inside and draw the water out.

Your wife is the same way. When you approach her, it's like reaching inside her heart and drawing out her affections. It's not, "Hey, Honey, turn on the water." You have to draw it out.

Proverbs 5:15 says, "Drink water from your own cistern, and running water from your own well." You have to draw out her affection and bring her to a place of sexual excitement and sexual fulfillment. It will always take her longer than it takes you. Set that in your mind now. The well is deep, and it takes time to draw it out.

I like to say it this way: STAY ABOVE THE BELT FOR AS LONG AS YOU CAN. Once we get married, everything speeds up. You're in a hurry. The kids are screaming for attention.

The television shouts "Watch me!" You have to get up early. You have to get some sleep.

You need to slow down. You like to go 50 mph. She needs to go 2 mph. Turn the television off a little earlier. Find an afternoon that's free. Take a weekend getaway. Find ways to make your world special.

If you've been on the fast track, tell your wife: "Honey, let's get away for a couple of days. Let's go practice great sex." Make a commitment to her that you will not have intercourse for at least one half hour once you start "stoking the fire." Give the fire time to spark. Give it time to burn. Do a lot of kissing and touching. Start from the toes up.

Now I know this sounds like a contradiction to what I just said about staying above the belt, but what I mean is, go slow. Take your time. Enjoy the whole person.

I've heard of an old Scottish marriage vow that says, "And in this marriage commitment, I will worship your body." The meaning of worship here is to reverence.[1] It means to have an innocence and purity in godly abandonment. This takes time, and it is the husband's job to slowly draw the wife to a place of passion.

Start with the toes and take a long time of just loving each other, enjoying what God has given to you in the physical realm of life. When you take the time to love one another like this, what is so valuable is that you reach a place of intimacy in your marriage where you completely give yourselves to each other. You have reached a part of your wife's heart or your husband's heart that no one else can ever touch. This kind of loving reaches a depth that nothing else can.

Remember, God's Word says, "Do not deprive one another except with consent for a time, that you may give yourselves to fasting and prayer; and come together again so that Satan does not tempt you because of your lack of self-control" (1 Cor. 7:5). When He said that, I believe He knew we would probably not fast for more than two or three days at a time. He recognized the need we have, and He put within us that need to come together in the physical realm in the marriage relationship.

This is truly being one flesh. Oneness is not just spiritual or just physical. It is a combination of the two.

True Sexual Fulfillment

Now, you husbands are completely different. The Bible describes you as a fountain. You just "go off"; climax is easy for you. Even if you're tired and have worked all day but see your wife take her clothes off, many times you instantly feel better and are aroused. You can have sex any time. But even if she sees you take off your shirt, many times nothing happens for her.

The reason may be that your wife is physically drained because she has worked all day or taken care of the kids and chased them around all day. You need to pitch in at home if you want good sex.

You may want your wife to work, to bring home a paycheck, and to do everything else around the house too. But if you want good sex, you've got to give her some time off so she can charge her physical and emotional batteries. If she's working five days a week and then coming home and working all evening as well, you will only get two days of her time. If she doesn't have any household help, then she alone has to do the laundry and other household chores, plus cook the meals, including getting up early to make the kids' breakfast. If that's the case, then you're down to one and a half days of her time. So you need to get up early once in awhile, make some breakfast for the kids, and get some laundry and other chores done. Then maybe you can both enjoy the physical aspect of your relationship more often.

First Peter 3:7-9 tells you:

> Husbands, likewise, dwell with them with understanding, giving honor to the wife, as to the weaker vessel, and as being heirs together of the grace of life, that your prayers may not be hindered.

Finally, all of you be of one mind, having compassion for one another; love as brothers, be tenderhearted, be courteous; not returning evil for evil or reviling for reviling, but on the contrary blessing, knowing that you were called to this, that you may inherit a blessing.

You have to dwell with your wife with understanding. Understand what she goes through. Understand her needs. Know how her spirit, soul, and body function. You have to realize that she is a well, and it takes time to draw her out.

Men, as long as you're breathing, climax for you is going to happen. Once you are stirred, it is easy for you physically to climax.

God painted the picture of a fountain in Proverbs 5:16, not me.

Husbands, make it last a little longer. Get romantic. Engage in foreplay. Be manly. Don't do it all in a few minutes, and before you know it, you're snoring, and your wife didn't even get started. This isn't meant to sound crude, but you're not twelve or fifteen years old anymore looking at a copy of a sex-oriented magazine in the backyard, and before you know it you are completely aroused, your "fountain" has gone off, and it's all over in seconds. It's time to realize this type of sex does not even come close to what God has offered you in the awesome celebration of your marriage. He has planned for husbands and wives to enjoy so much more.

Sure, you and your wife can play around and just have fun. You can "take a little spin around the block," spend a few minutes together, have sex, and not take a long time. There are all kinds of sex. There's what I call breakfast, lunch, dinner, and snacks. To me, snacks are like a "spin around the block," where she may not climax, but you both have fun. But you can't live off snacks. Breakfast and lunch are fun, too—not too light, not too heavy—but you can't live off those either.

You have to have a healthy sexual diet of full course meals—dinner out on the town, so to speak, where it's a nice, slow time of intimacy. I believe that the best sexual diet is to mix it all up. Don't let it be the same all the time. Realize that with snacks and light meals, she may not climax, and that's okay. You both have to have dinner regularly, but she should climax consistently too. There has to be a commitment on the part of the husband to "draw out of the well" continuously.

I encourage you to heed Proverbs 5:16,17 as well: "Should your fountains be dispersed abroad, streams of water in the streets? Let them be only your own, and not for strangers with you." In other words, don't give your "fountain" to any woman on the street. Don't give your "fountain" to the girl in the magazine or the girl on the Internet, as we talked about earlier.

If you like having cybersex (on the Internet), sex through sex-oriented magazines or movies, or sex through masturbation, it is very possible that you consider your own being worthless. You may consider your sexual intimacy to be cheap. So you throw it away, trying to find sexual fulfillment everywhere but with your wife, and it means nothing to you.

I have heard it said that if a man has a little self-esteem, he won't sleep around. If he has a little self-recognition of who he is as a man of God, he won't hold back from being intimate with his wife. In other words, he won't keep his pants on for the wife who is worthy.

Husbands, take the time, be patient, slow down, and connect with your wife. Think about how you are going to satisfy and fulfill your wife. If your wife has never been sexually fulfilled or sexual orgasm is not a normal part of her life, you have to get to work.

It's not a question of your "manliness." It's about your marriage, your love, and your commitment to your wife. "But I don't know what to do," you may say. Talk to her. Ask her, "Honey, what should I change in my lovemaking with you?"

It may be that all you need to do is take a shower. And it may be hard for her to get excited when you can't breathe through your nose.

Sometimes husbands and wives don't tell each other the truth. They lie and fake. If your wife has perfume on that makes you gag, just tell her, but say it nicely: "Honey, I really don't care for that perfume. Could you buy some other kind?" Or surprise her by buying her a new bottle of a fragrance that you like. If your husband has worn the same after-shave lotion for thirty years, you could say something like, "Honey, you can water the plants with that, but please don't wear it around me." Or give him a gift of a new men's cologne that excites you whenever you smell it.

You have to be honest. You have to start talking to each other. Help each other so that you can enjoy your sex life. Help each other find sex fulfilling and rewarding.

"But my wife just won't talk," you may say.

It's just possible that something has happened, and she's given up. If that's the case, tell her, "Honey, I want to start over. Let's put some fluid in the transmission and keep this thing from burning up. Let's figure out what to do together."

Wives, sex means something completely different to your husband than it does to you. Like a woman, it does satisfy his sex drive—but his drive is different than yours.

In Tim and Beverly LaHaye's book *The Act of Marriage,* which I referenced earlier, they explain a man's sex drive physiologically and how a man could have sex multiple times a day, depending on his age. The male body produces hormones that are building within all the time. So it creates a tremendous sex drive.[2]

You may say, "Oh, my husband never wants to have sex." Then you do have a very unique situation. Be careful not to put your husband down. He needs wisdom and perhaps healing.

Think about all of this. If a man can have sex every half hour and come to climax every time, then he has to have some strength. His sex drive is not abnormal. He's not filled with "the lust of the flesh" (1 John 2:16). God made him the way he is. If we were to survey the neighborhood and ask married couples how many times they had sex this week, we would find out that our husbands are average. So don't put your husband down or attack his ego.

God made his ego, too, for your benefit, and sex fulfills your husband's ego. Men were created to be the protectors, the drivers, and the go-getters. Some women have taken it upon themselves to crush those qualities and let them know they need to be meek, humble men of God.

Yes, they are to be meek, humble men of God, but that has nothing to do with pulling down their ego. A fulfilling sex life does something to the male ego. Build your husband's up. Building their ego gives them the strength to do more in achieving their goals. It will increase their drive to succeed in life. You have the power to strengthen their self-image.

Sex enhances the husband's love for his wife, and it reduces friction and squabbling in the home. The tenderness of your love for him, satisfying his sexual drive, and building his ego will cause him to love and admire you more. He will respond to your love and admiration for him.

In their book *The Act of Marriage,* Tim and Beverly LaHaye talk about how one woman figured out that her husband was always irritable on one particular day of the month.[3] She finally realized that on that day he always did the bills at work. So she got smart.

She made sure they had sex the night before and the night after. She said it was the only way she could get him back to his normal self because the worry and fear of not succeeding as a man began to take control of his mind.

Have you ever noticed something like this with your husband? Are there times when he gets edgy? You may think he is mad or upset with you, but it's probably much deeper.

Even though women can do almost anything a man can do regarding salaries and careers, they don't have the same makeup as the protector and provider that God made men to be.

Have you ever thought of how your husband feels the night before he has a big presentation or a new job interview for a promotion? He's probably nervous.

Minister to him. Being a wife is a ministry. Be wise. Give yourself to your husband, and assist him in actually flowing in the power of God. Doesn't that sound unique? It is amazing what your ministry to him can do.

Before a huge game, as a boxing match or a football game, coaches never let their players be with their wives. They don't want their players to get rid of the edge—the friction. They want them to be mean and nasty so they'll win.

I heard one woman say once concerning her relationship with her husband, "We've got to have sex again. My husband is getting too nasty."

I think it would be easier to give yourself freely and frequently so that he never becomes nasty. Pull down the friction in your home by the sweetness that comes through the celebration of love.

Sex is the most exciting experience a man can have in his life, and it is the most earthshaking, wonderful experience he can think of when it is with you.

Wives, if you really don't know what to do, if you really don't know how to find a place of sexual fulfillment, and your husband doesn't know what to do, do what the Bible says:

> the older women likewise, that they be reverent in behavior, not slanderers, not given to much wine, teachers of good things;
>
> that they admonish the young women to love their husbands, to love their children,
>
> to be discreet, chaste, homemakers, good, obedient to their own husbands, that the word of God may not be blasphemed.
>
> Titus 2:3-5

Go to an older woman. Find a woman who looks as if she has good sex with her husband. Try talking to your pastor's wife, the elders' wives, or your Bible study leader. Find someone who teaches on these matters. Say to them, "My husband and I are struggling with our sexual relationship. Can you help me? Could you give me some ideas?" We are all human. No one is going to say, "What? You don't know what to do?"

You aren't born with the knowledge. I know I'm talking to wives about asking for help, but men, you don't know how to have good sex just because you are a man. You need help too.

Love Your Frame

Now, men, there's more to the Proverbs 5 passage for you. Verse 19 says, "As a loving deer and a graceful doe, let her breasts satisfy you at all times; and always be enraptured with her love."

Be satisfied with your wife's breasts. Galatians 6:7,8 apply to every area of our lives: "Do not be deceived, God is not mocked; for whatever a man sows, that he will also reap. For he who sows to his flesh will of the flesh reap corruption, but he who sows to the Spirit will of the Spirit reap everlasting life."

If you sow destruction in your marriage, you will reap destruction. If you sow your life against the principles of the Word of God, you will reap destruction of your life.

Hebrews 13:4,5 admonish us: "Marriage is honorable among all, and the bed undefiled; but fornicators and adulterers God will judge. Let your conduct be without covetousness; be content with such things as you have...."

Men, don't covet the breasts or body shapes of other women. Don't say or think, "I wish my wife looked like that woman." Women, don't say, "I wish my husband had that." Don't wish he were broader or taller.

Wishing your wife had what another woman does is coveting what someone else has and wanting it in your realm of life. It's having vain imaginations of the way you want your mate to look.

Second Corinthians 10:4,5 say we're to pull down strongholds; we're to cast down imaginations and everything that exalts itself against the knowledge of God:

> For the weapons of our warfare are not carnal but mighty in God for pulling down strongholds,
>
> casting down arguments and every high thing that exalts itself against the knowledge of God, bringing every thought into captivity to the obedience of Christ.

Remember the story of the gentleman who opened my doors and carried my packages? I coveted his actions. I wanted Casey to be like him. He turned out to be a real disappointment when he ran off with the church secretary. I certainly didn't want Casey to be like that. I was wrong. Since those early years of marriage, Casey has become a wonderful gentleman. He is always doing special things for me.

Be careful because what you covet is not always what it seems to be. We only see tiny parts when we're looking at how green the grass looks "over there." If we'll get a little closer, we'll see all the cow patties scattered around. Be content with what you have.

David wrote in Psalm 139, "I will praise You, for I am fearfully and wonderfully made; marvelous are Your works, and that my soul knows very well. My frame was not hidden from You, when I was made in secret, and skillfully wrought in the lowest parts of the earth" (vv. 14,15).

God made your wife's frame. God made your husband's frame. God doesn't want all of us to look identical. God didn't make one size frame and exclaim, "Oh, that's My favorite. I'll make millions." No. We are not all supposed to have long limbs or all short limbs. We aren't all supposed to have big hips or all little hips. We aren't all supposed to have little heads or big heads or big breasts or little breasts.

Women, love your frame. God made it. It is not a mistake. If you're tall, you're supposed to be tall. If you're short, you're supposed to be short.

Men, love your wife's frame. God made it. It is not a mistake. Don't wish she had bigger breasts. I've heard so many comments on breast size through the years, and they are all so ignorant. Breast tissue is just fat. God made each woman with the right amount of fat. So, receive it. Love her frame. Don't covet another kind of frame. Let her breasts satisfy you at all times.

One day I turned on the television, and there was a counselor talking with a married couple on a talk show. The husband was complaining, before millions of viewers, about how he no longer liked the top half of his wife's body.

The counselor was bold enough and courageous enough to say, "You mean you're complaining after she's had two of your children, and the reason that she doesn't look like she did when you married her is that she nursed your children? Your babies did that to her. Your children did that, and you're complaining?"

What that counselor said needed to be said. That man, and men like him, need to get it together.

Men, I am writing this to you because at every women's conference where I speak, and at the weekly Bible study at our church, I tell the women to love their husbands, honor them, submit to them, to love who you are, embrace who you are, and the gifting that you have. It's hard for them to do that if you aren't doing your part.

Men, when you are discontented with your wife and compare her to other women, you affect her whole personhood. When you look at sexually oriented magazines or movies or at sexually explicit Web sites on the Internet, your actions say that you are discontent. You sow seeds of insecurity into your wife—and then wonder why she feels no freedom with you in the bedroom. You shut the door.

Now, if you want to open the door, clean up your mind and your heart. Change your actions. Start loving the frame that God has given to your wife.

Watch what you say. Don't correct her in the bedroom. Men or women who do this have a controlling attitude. Yes, you have to communicate about what you like and don't like, but be gentle. Watch your timing.

Not only do we have to be careful of how we communicate in the bedroom, but at other times as well. I know all about this one. I am one of the most guilty, and I work very hard at becoming better. I'm learning to have the right timing to communicate. I used to think I needed to say everything the minute I saw my husband come through the front door.

I don't know how many times I've thought, *Oh, I should have waited. I could have waited five or ten minutes. I could have waited until tomorrow. I should have thought it through a little bit more.*

Be very sensitive. Before you open your mouth, think about how many kind words you've said lately. How much have you comforted? How sensitive have you been to what's been going on with your kids? Do you know what time of the month it is?

Yes, men, you have to stay in touch with that too. I love the story of the man who lived in a house with his wife and seven daughters. Once a month, he simply opened the door and threw chocolate in. It was the safest move he could make.

Seriously, be aware of your wife and what's going on in her life emotionally and physically. Cultivate your love and relationship. Recognize your differences as a man and a woman. Be gentle and kind. Learn to understand how each of you thinks and is created to respond. All of the effort you put forth will be worth it. Your relationship will flourish and so will your sex life.

New Thoughts to Think

To deprive your mate of sex is not your decision to make. It is to be a mutual agreement between husband and wife for the purpose of fasting and prayer. Ask the Holy Spirit to guide you together—as husband and wife—to set aside special time for fasting and prayer, yet being sensitive to each other so as to not deprive each other sexually.

6

Wisdom From the Prostitute

It's comforting to know that God left nothing out in teaching us how to be married and live peaceably together. He has given us kind directives and clear insights.

I love to study the differences between right and wrong, the colorful pictures that the Lord paints for us in the Scriptures. For example, He teaches us about a godly wife, and then reveals to us the heart and behavior of a prostitute. We can learn volumes from both.

Several verses in Proverbs 7 show us how a prostitute gets her man. Her tactics are shrewd and purposeful. We can learn what we might be doing ourselves that is inappropriate from studying what she does, as well as where we need to pay more attention.

> And there a woman met him, with the attire of a harlot, and a crafty heart.

She was loud and rebellious, her feet would not stay at home.

I have spread my bed with tapestry, Colored coverings of Egyptian linen.

I have perfumed my bed with myrrh, aloes, and cinnamon.

Come, let us take our fill of love until morning; let us delight ourselves with love.

With her enticing speech she caused him to yield, with her flattering lips she seduced him.

PROVERBS 7:10,11,16-18,21

The *King James Version* of verse 11 describes the prostitute as loud, stubborn, and "her feet abide not in her house." This says more than you realize.

This spirit lives in too many Christian women's lives. They busy themselves so much that they are always tired or too busy for their husbands. They are on every committee, teach three home meetings, go to two Bible studies, sing in the choir, and are the room mother for all their children.

Her feet abide not in her house.

Now, of course, you aren't to lock yourself in twenty-four hours a day, seven days a week. That would be ridiculous. But consider your activities. Ask yourself the question: "What can I do to keep myself fresh, alert, and ready for my husband?" That's not just for his sexual needs but for the whole lifestyle of your home.

When Casey and I were first married, and when we didn't have children, we could stay up until 2:00 A.M. and sleep in until 10:00 A.M. We simply unplugged the phone and no one interrupted us. We could stay up late, working out issues in our marriage or whatever we wanted to do. We could adjust our schedule however we wanted it. Once we had children, there were more demands on our time. We had to change some of the ways we lived. I had many different responsibilities, and I didn't want to give those up. When we started our church, most of the people didn't think I could do anything. I set out to prove them wrong. Finally, I had to recognize, *Wendy, what you are doing right now is trying to prove your value to other people. You are not looking after your husband to minister to him.*

My feet were not staying home. I had to look at my motivation and priorities. I realized that I did not want to be a woman who was always running away, trying to earn my self-image, my self-worth, establishing who I was by all the things I did outside of the gifts God had invested in me.

We have to realize that there is a real push on us to continuously be superwomen. It is very easy to be so busy in your life that you actually are unfulfilled as a woman. You are not doing what is truly in your heart to do. It is easy to find millions of projects to do because there is always someone who will call you and ask you to do something.

I still work many hours each week coordinating and overseeing areas of our ministry, but I'm not in charge of practically everything as I once was.

A wise and virtuous woman prays, asks God, and considers a responsibility before she takes it on. Without God's wisdom, you will be too tired to give yourself to your husband.

A virtuous woman submits from her own heart because of love. I believe a woman who works full time must be wise in her schedule if she has children and a husband.

The woman who works full time and then goes home and tries to clean her four-bedroom house should have a housekeeper. The woman in Proverbs 31:15 NIV had help: "She gets up while it is still dark; she provides food for her family and portions for her servant girls."

Let's say you come home from work at 5:00 P.M., and you have to make dinner for two children and a husband. You finish cleaning up the kitchen by 6:30 P.M. Then you have to run a couple of loads of laundry, help your children with their homework, and pack their lunches for the next day. Later, you collapse into bed.

The next morning you inhale breakfast and out the door you go. You didn't get to vacuuming, cleaning the bathrooms, or dusting. You didn't even get to sit down. This is an example of a woman who lacks wisdom with her time and planning. Her feet are not staying at home, even though she is at home.

You have to be wise with your time. You must evaluate all the things in which you are involved. Ask yourself, "Is it wise for my family and for my relationship with my husband?" Time, laziness, tiredness, and many responsibilities will keep you from being stirred up sexually.

The prostitute runs all over the place, and she's loud. Loud has to do with having an air of loudness about her. From what I read in *Strong's Exhaustive Concordance of the Bible,* I see loudness as always expressing your opinion, fighting, and causing friction and tension because you insist on your own way.[1] It's a stubborn spirit that says, "I'm doing what I want to do. Don't you tell me what to do."

A Bible Wife vs. a New Millennium Wife

First Peter 3:1,2 KJV is God's instruction to godly wives. It paints a very different picture from the prostitute and her ways.

> Likewise, ye wives, be in subjection to your own husbands; that, if any obey not the word, they also may without the word be won by the conversation of the wives;
>
> While they behold your chaste conversation coupled with fear.

Today, more than ever, many women fight against a biblical type of marriage. The Bible isn't a new millennium book. It's a book of truths that never changes, generation after generation.

Sometimes the Bible conflicts with our personal point of view. When this occurs, we want to rise up, become irritated, and feel belittled and insignificant. Low self-esteem will try to rise up and fight. We do not always see ourselves as God does. The more we see ourselves as God does, the less we feel we have to fight for "our rights," for honor, or for our identity as women.

Here's a suggestion: When you feel like fighting, write your thoughts down. This will help you identify the areas where you need the Spirit of God to walk you through. Ask God to teach you in these areas. Ask God to help you sort through all you feel. He is your strength, and you need to rely on Him to help you change.

In *The Living Bible,* 1 Peter 3:1,2 reads: "Wives, fit in with your husbands' plans; for then if they refuse to listen when you talk to them about the Lord, they will be won by your respectful, pure behavior. Your godly lives will speak to them better than any words."

Too often, we think our husbands won't change unless we tell them repeatedly about an area that needs change. For instance, if he doesn't pick up his socks, we become irritated, feel like a slave, and talk to him about it repeatedly.

Stop talking. Proverbs 21:19 says, "Better to dwell in the wilderness, than with a contentious and angry woman." You are not your husband's Holy Spirit. Make a decision: "I will not talk about it again."

God's Word has a way to make things work. The Word applied gives us success in marriage instead of failure. The Word teaches us the perfect way to make things wonderful in our home.

Simply put, *The Living Bible* says to fit in with your husband's plans—not talk to him. Your godly life will speak louder to him than your words. If you want him to change, put yourself into your husband's plan—and his plan is not to pick up his socks.

At the same time, many of us have been trained to disregard all authority. That is not scriptural. The Word talks about understanding and living correctly under authority. (Luke 7:7-9; Matt. 8:9; 1 Tim. 2:1,2.) I have found that to live free and walk in the place God has called me to is to come under authority with my thoughts, my rebellion, my irritations, and my laziness. Try it—see what happens.

Coming under authority in marriage means we are to be submissive to our husband. (Eph. 5:22.) That is part of God's design for marriage.[2] Now, notice that I'm not saying submission to men, rather submission to your own husband. Your husband is different than any other man on earth. I yield to my husband's plans, and I submit to the godly direction and wisdom in him.

I understand that many husbands may want to do some things that aren't God's direction, but if they are morally right, you are to submit.

However, if your husband asks you to do something such as go to a party with ten other couples, and they are all having sex together, don't go. Don't be what the Bible calls a "silly" woman. (2 Tim. 3:6 KJV.) Don't be silly and conned into such things. Never honor anything anyone says if it goes against the Word of God.

The Word of God is what you submit to first, and then your husband. You can obey everything your husband asks as long as it doesn't contradict the Bible.

To be submissive is to be subordinate.[3] A submissive wife's first reaction is to obey, to give, and to jump in there. To yield and submit is a personal choice. We as women have a personal choice to decide to be a submissive woman, and we will bear fruit of the choice we make.

If you yield, honor, and give up your own selfish way for your husband's way, you will reap the same from him. He will prefer and honor you.

Peter's words in 1 Peter 3:1,2 TLB challenge you in your attitude and rights: "...they will be won by your respectful, pure behavior. Your godly lives will speak to them better than any words." These verses challenge you in your irritations and your thoughts. To get the benefits of God's Word, we have to give up our way and take on God's way. That means, "My reflex is to obey. My understanding must be in a subordinate type of thought."

It is a choice to allow yourself to yield to your husband's plan. The word "submit" is the same word used in the way you should act toward God and toward your church. We're to submit to God, to our husbands, and to the church. (Eph. 5:22-25.)

When your spirit is in line with the Word, you will bear fruit in your life.

Throw Away the Orange Lipstick

Not everyone had a mother, aunts, or grandmothers who knew how to dress like godly women and passed that wisdom on to the next generation. Sometimes we all need instruction in what is appropriate for a godly woman to wear. We need information about what are the best colors to wear, the best makeup, or the best styles for our frame. We don't need to dress or appear like the prostitute.

Too many Christian women unknowingly do just that.

The Word of God is what we should base our dress and appearance on. It is God's taste, and it is always appropriate.

Let's look at some Scriptures that touch on this subject.

> Whose adorning let it not be that outward adorning of plaiting the hair, and of wearing of gold, or of putting on of apparel;
>
> But let it be the hidden man of the heart, in that which is not corruptible, even the ornament of a meek and quiet spirit, which is in the sight of God of great price.
>
> For after this manner in the old time the holy women also, who trusted in God, adorned themselves, being in subjection unto their own husbands:
>
> Even as Sara obeyed Abraham, calling him lord: whose daughters ye are, as long as ye do well, and are not afraid with any amazement.
>
> 1 PETER 3:3-6 KJV

Proverbs 31:11 AMP says: "The heart of her husband trusts in her confidently and relies on and believes in her securely, so that he has no lack of [honest] gain or need of [dishonest] spoil."

Proverbs 31:22,30 KJV instruct us: "She maketh herself coverings of tapestry; her clothing is silk and purple.

Favour is deceitful, and beauty is vain: but a woman that feareth the LORD, she shall be praised."

Verse 30 in *The Amplified Bible* reads, "Charm and grace are deceptive, and beauty is vain [because it is not lasting], but a woman who reverently and worshipfully fears the Lord, she shall be praised!"

The instruction in 1 Peter 3 about a godly woman's attire is clear. It's not an outward adorning but rather the hidden inner person of the heart. Proverbs 31 says, "a virtuous woman" dresses in beautiful clothing and silk. From these Scriptures, I want you to understand that it's not the outward dress that your mate is looking for, although a virtuous woman does dress herself beautifully.

Too often Christian women act ignorantly about dress. In the work place, a godly woman should not wear clothing designed to "turn a man on." We are not supposed to turn on every man. We are to turn on only one—our husband. We need to be chaste, holy, and pure in how we look.

The prostitute is the one who dresses to get a man. She is a loose woman who dresses to attract all men to herself. She knows what will turn a man's head and what will turn him on. That is her business. She is sly, cunning of heart, and crafty. Her entire motive is to get a man.

If a woman does this, her motive is self-oriented; it's selfish like the harlot. All she wants from the man is his money and his life. Her motive is not based on love, as 1 Peter 3 describes. A wife's motive should be based on love. When you dress to draw attention to yourself, it reveals your insecurity. You want attention—the wrong kind of attention.

Women look at each other differently than men do. We look at each other and think, *She looks good.* But we don't think that in a sexual sense. We typically look at men who are trying to impress us and think, *Who are you doing this for? What a turnoff.* Men with their shirts unbuttoned and their chests covered in gold chains typically don't do a thing for us.

Men are attracted by physical appearance. They do think sexually when they look at a woman, especially if she is wiggling her behind or wearing a low-cut blouse.

A holy, virtuous woman needs to think about what she does to men. Don't wear tight clothes to work. Yet, don't go to the other extreme and dress unattractively. Don't live in your sweatshirts or T-shirts. The point is, don't be flirtatious with any man other than your husband.

When you shop, consider if the latest fashions are godly, and show your inner qualities as a mighty woman of God. Ask yourself these two questions before you really think a fashion is hip: 1) Does it look godly, and 2) does it allow me to really be myself?

Your Husband Will Be Attracted to Someone—Make Sure It's You

The other side of the story is, as Christian women we need to study the ways of the prostitute and learn from her. The prostitute plans how she is going to get her man. She is attractive. She takes time to be ready, willing, and available for him.

Proverbs 7:16,17 tell us the prostitute gets everything in the bedroom ready by making it pretty and attractive to the eye. Men are attracted by what they see, and they are attracted by what they smell. Christian women would do well to pay attention to this. Sometimes we use the same sheets on the bed that we've used for ten years because we don't want to spend money. That isn't wise.

I realize your husband may be attracted to you no matter what, especially in your sexual relationship. But it is necessary to invest in yourself to not only attract him, but to keep him fired up.

Sometimes we do little to nothing to entice, allure, or keep those fires kindled in our husband's heart toward us. The devil wants to attack him and shift his affection to the wrong person. We must be smart enough to use the wisdom of the world against the world to show they can't win.

I love the example God gave us in the Bible of Queen Esther. God used Esther to save her people from destruction. In order to be used in this situation, Esther had to do specific things first. She took time to prepare herself physically before she went before the king. (Est. 2:12.) She prepared her body and clothing. She was beautiful, and when the time came, she was ready to go before him. (Est. 2:15.)

Many of us just don't take the time to think and prepare for our husband. When he sees that you have taken the time to get ready for him, you have his heart in the palm of your hand.

One of my friends told me she wears leopard or zebra underwear. No one knows she wears such except her husband. She calls him sometimes during the day and says, "I've got my zebra on."

She's smart. She's stirring him up.

Keep yourself attractive. Take care of yourself. Be clean and neat. Wear the colors that are best for you. If you don't know what those are, seek wisdom from a friend or salon. Learn to apply your makeup properly. Don't wear the same thing you wore when you were sixteen years old.

As a teen, I wore silver eye shadow from my eyelashes to my eyebrows and orange lipstick. That was probably appropriate for my age and the current fashion trends of the late 70s, but I had to move on and change with the times. It's good to wear makeup, but we have to wear it correctly and make sure our heart is right.

I've heard some women say that they won't go outside or let their husbands see them without their makeup on. To me, that is low-self esteem. In their hearts, these women say, *I'm not beautiful enough to be seen without my makeup on.* Your natural state is beautiful. God made you that way.

Now, if you don't know how to apply makeup in a way that is most attractive for your features, ask for help at the cosmetic counters at the store. They will apply it for free and teach you techniques.

Likewise, hair stylists at salons will teach you how to wear your hair in an attractive style. You can learn how to make yourself an attractive, beautiful Christian woman. A virtuous woman's motive is not to sexually attract men; it is to attract A MAN—her husband—and to glorify her heavenly Father.

So prepare yourself to look and smell beautiful for your husband to attract him to you, and he won't look anywhere else. Wear the right attire for all the right occasions. If you're going to a Christmas party where there will be fine china and beautiful decorations, don't show up in sweats and tennis shoes—even if your shirt does say, "Jesus is the Reason." Select one of your favorite dresses and matching shoes. Spend extra time applying your makeup and styling your hair.

The point here is, stay prepared and ready. From my conversations with men and women over the years, it seems many women don't think about sex during the day, yet it seems men generally think about it at least once a day. Be smart, sexy, fun loving, party going, and wise. Be ready for the party that you want your husband to attend—the love celebration for just the two of you.

Work on That Inner Beauty

As godly women, we need to really emphasize the inner beauty over the outward adornment. It's great to know your colors and how to apply makeup, but don't lower your thoughts of your marriage to the level of how you look on the outside. Marriage is a covenant relationship. Your husband made a covenant to God first and to you second. If he breaks that covenant, God will judge him.

If you have to look a certain way for your husband or do things to please him, pray for God to change his heart and how he sees you. In the meantime, continue to work on your inner beauty. It will shine through.

Remember, the outside can be a very beautiful picture, but there needs to be a balance. The inside can be a skeleton that is ugly, undone, jealous, envious, undisciplined, hateful, bitter, and hurt. If you're like that on the inside, those qualities will appear in your marriage.

Today there is a real sense of "I have to have my physical body just right." You may exercise for the outward beauty but not exercise for health and long life. If you are constantly consumed with how you look, you need to overcome this.

If you have an eating disorder and are consumed with how you look, ask God to give you the strength to overcome, to come out of this place of bondage. The devil is the one who wants to keep you in a place of bondage, where you will never truly have the heart of a submitted woman because your heart and mind are consumed with yourself. A woman like this doesn't allow any room in her heart to love and honor anyone else. She is consumed with her low self-esteem.

If you want a great marriage, work on your inner beauty—and one quality that will enhance your inner beauty is to trust in God. Know who He is. Read His Word. Develop the inner beauty of your heart.

First Peter 3:4,5 in *The Living Bible* says, "Be beautiful inside, in your hearts, with the lasting charm of a gentle and quiet spirit that is so precious to God. That kind of deep beauty was seen in the saintly women of old, who trusted God and fitted in with their husbands' plans."

It's never too late to grow, change, and renew. No one is perfect, but we can all be challenged to look at where we need to grow, and then train ourselves according to God's Word.

Train yourself to be a Bible wife, not a new millennium wife who is hip on all the world's ways and fashions. Make a decision to grow to respect, reverence, notice, regard, honor, prefer, venerate, esteem, defer to, praise, love, and admire your husband exceedingly. (Eph. 5:33 AMP.)

New Thoughts to Think

Evaluate your priorities and make sure your feet are staying at home appropriately so that you can be fresh, alert, and ready for your husband and for the lifestyle of your home. Ask God for wisdom in this area, and don't be afraid to bow out of some of your present responsibilities.

Ask the Lord how to renew your inner beauty, first, to glorify Him, and second, to please your husband. Develop a gentle and peaceful spirit. (1 Pet. 3:4.)

Ask the Lord how He would have you keep the love fires kindled in your husband's heart toward you. Consider Proverbs 31:12 AMP: "She comforts, encourages, and does him [her husband] only good as long as there is life within her."

7

Nurturing Your Mate
and Your Marriage

When you marry, you can't expect a perfect husband, although many women do. Their feet barely touch the ground because they are so "in love." They walk on air, skipping from cloud to cloud.

In time, the routine of life enables them to touch earth, and they discover their knight in shining armor has a few flaws. They begin to mention his flaws, ever so gently at first, until a full-scale assault is ensued. There are numerous ways of waging marital wars in an effort to change your mate, but no matter what you've tried, there is a biblical way.

Galatians 6:7,8 tells us that we reap what we sow. If you want to reap love in its fullest capacity from your mate, you have to sow it. The more you sow, the more you will reap.

When you want your spouse to change in an area, you won't see results if you control, manipulate, or dominate. You sow. When you sow, you are actually nurturing your marriage relationship. You empower it to grow and become all that God wants it to be—and all that you want it to be.

The following are several demonstrations of love you can sow into your spouse to reap a more fulfilling relationship in the bedroom and outside the bedroom. They all help to build up to passionate sexual love.

Companionship

Women want male companionship. They want someone they can talk to and share with. At the same time, women must be responsible to help their husbands understand how to be their companions.

Although you will find men who tend to be hermits and loners, you won't find as many women with that same tendency. Men are more comfortable not talking at times. It's often been said that men are *headliners* and women are *detailers.*

Nonetheless, you can nurture your husband and help him learn how to be your companion. Begin with a date. Sit down and talk to him. Even if you're thinking, *My husband doesn't want to talk to me,* be creative in your ways of getting him to talk to you. Take advantage of times when he's relaxed, when he'll enjoy your conversation.

Some women want the companionship first. They want their husband to give to them first. You need to work with your mate. Be willing to give to him first. Be willing to sow into his life and care about him first. Then you will reap what you have sown.

Luke 6:38 says, "Give, and it will be given to you: good measure, pressed down, shaken together, and running over will be put into your bosom. For with the same measure that you use, it will be measured back to you."

Not all men know how to be a companion, but you can nurture your relationship where your husband can easily begin to draw close to you.

One way I've engaged Casey in conversation and drawn him into companionship has been to keep our conversations interesting. If he started to read a magazine or do something else, I just kept talking. Eventually, he could not read and listen to me, so one had to go. If I continued to make conversation more interesting than the magazine, he wanted to listen to me.

That meant I couldn't just be shooting my mouth off or idly blabbering, which we as women sometimes are guilty of doing. Instead, I usually started with a great story, something that the kids had done. Casey usually put down his magazine, said "Really?" and then laughed.

I usually answered, "Yeah, and you know what else?" and off I went. Today he loves listening and talking to me. It's like a realm he never knew until I nurtured it in our relationship. I didn't control, manipulate, or demand. I loved him and wooed him into loving conversations about our lives, what went on during the day, and issues that might be on my mind. Well, actually, I did manipulate, demand, and control at times, but I am working on this. It has cultivated a relationship between us that has opened the door for him to share with me. It has made us close companions.

Compassionate Love

Compassionate love is not sexual love. It is sweetness and thoughtfulness. It's saying, "I love you." It's speaking with kind words, offering a helping hand, doing something before he has the time to ask. It's serving and giving of your time and abilities. It's listening attentively and looking at him in the eyes when he talks to you. It's dropping what you're doing and giving him your full attention. It extends from a heart that is soft and pliable, from a heart of love.

If you will be a compassionate lover, then you will receive the same kind of love in return.

Romantic Love

Romantic love encompasses gift giving, opening the doors, buying flowers, and doing other special things. Some husbands seem to do these things easily. If yours doesn't, don't be angry with him. Instead, nurture your relationship with your husband with patience. There have been times when I've gone out to the car and just stood by my door. Casey has gotten in the car and then caught himself. He's jumped back out of the car, run around it, and opened my door. If yours does this, say something sweet when he gets back in like, "Oh, sweetheart, thank you." Don't be critical. Criticism never nurtures.

Affection

Affection is kissing and hugging, rather than sex. Husbands often don't understand this need. Some of them don't need a lot of the kind of hugging and kissing a woman wants. If you hug and kiss a man, he's ready to go sexually, but a woman just needs the affection.

Creatively Cultivate Your Love

Love can be expressed in so many ways—compassionate ways, romantic ways, and affectionate ways. In general, it takes a balance of all these ways, but we all have areas where we are stronger than others.

Personally, I am not very good at remembering to buy gifts for Casey. I have to work at buying gifts, being romantic, getting him cards and balloons, and all the fun things. Sometimes it is difficult to follow through on my intentions because I don't think about these things as often as I should.

We all have our high points, and remembering all of these things isn't one of mine. We must understand there are areas our husbands have not cultivated.

For example, you might try to get your husband to be a great companion who is compassionate, romantic, affectionate, and passionate and wind up beating your head against a brick wall. One of these qualities is probably not going to be his high point.

Your husband might be rated an A+ in one quality. He might be the most wonderful companion. You simply couldn't ask for a better "best buddy." He knows how to talk and share, but when it comes to affection, kissing, and hugging, he might hit zero.

So what? Understand your kind of man, and then allow him to be himself. Nurture him in that area of your relationship.

There are different kinds of personalities—the lover, the meditator, the driver, and the promoter to name a few. Discern your man, and you will see his strengths as well as his weaknesses. Don't beat yourself trying to make him conform, but instead, allow him to develop these characteristics to the fullest. You will encourage that development by understanding your husband.

There are many ways you can keep the fire stoked in your marriage and encourage the development of these qualities in your mate.

As I said earlier, you can give. You have to give if you want to receive. Give companionship. Give compassionate love. Give romantic love, affection, and passion. You don't necessarily have to give them in this order, but you do need to be the instigator.

Remember Luke 6:38? Give, and it shall be given to you. Whatever measure you give out, it's going to be measured back to you again.

A Scripture that goes along with this is Galatians 6:7-10, which says:

> Do not be deceived, God is not mocked; for whatever a man sows, that he will also reap.
>
> For he who sows to his flesh will of the flesh reap corruption, but he who sows to the Spirit will of the Spirit reap everlasting life.
>
> And let us not grow weary while doing good, for in due season we shall reap if we do not lose heart.

Therefore, as we have opportunity, let us do good to all, especially to those who are of the household of faith.

If you continually reap anger and bitterness from your husband, check out what you sow into his life. Now I'm not referring to abuse here. As I said earlier, if you are in an abusive situation, get help immediately. But you may have an angry, bitter attitude that you give vent to with your husband. If you've recently been saved and your husband is not saved, you will need to work these negative qualities out of your life before you expect them not to be expressed in his life.

Just Talk

Talk honestly. Have a regularly planned time to talk with your husband. Casey and I date regularly. When we do, we spend two to four hours just talking.

Sure, we talk each day, but I'm talking about time set aside for us alone. You may say, "Well, my husband doesn't want to go out with me." You can encourage and love your husband to do anything you want. I believe that sometimes we give ourselves excuses to get out of things instead of instigate love.

"We don't have any time to go out," you may say.

The truth is, you aren't any busier than anyone else. You have to make it happen. Casey and I have to make it happen. Our relationship is why we are able to do anything in this life—our relationship with each other and with God. Our relationship is strong, but it isn't going to stay strong if we don't cultivate it.

I'm no fool. The devil comes all the time to steal, kill, and destroy our relationship—and everything else. Jesus said it would be that way: "The thief does not come except to steal, and to kill, and to destroy. I have come that they may have life, and that they may have it more abundantly" (John 10:10).

"Yeah, but we don't have any money to go out," you may say.

Then pack a lunch and go to the beach or the park. Sit on a blanket and talk for hours. If it's cold or rainy, go to the mall with your lunch and sit on the benches and talk. Spend only four or five dollars on a muffin and a bowl of soup...and talk. Just talk.

Change Yourself First

Change always begins one step at a time. Work on the different points you've learned in this book, and take it one step at a time. I know you want your husband to be compassionate, romantic, nice, and affectionate, but you be the first to change. Recognize that your relationship didn't become what it is right now with one partner. You have sown into it, and he has sown into it. Now it's time for you both to change and to sow the right things into your relationship.

In thinking about becoming romantic and compassionate, remember what sex means to a man. It satisfies his sexual drive, fulfills his male ego, enhances his love for you, reduces friction in the home, and provides the most exciting experience in his life. If the greatest area you need to change is to have sex more often, then do it. Afterwards, work on developing the other characteristics.

Loosen Up

As you begin to change yourself, think about ways you can present yourself as a beautiful lady. Be a lady around your husband. Act ladylike. Walk ladylike. Sit ladylike. When you are out with your husband, act like a lady, and he will see you like a lady. Work to change every area of your life to become ladylike.

Some women are too serious-minded. Loosen up. Everything becomes a drag when it is all so important. Take the time to laugh at life and have fun.

When your husband comes home, don't tell him every negative thing of the day right away. That is inconsiderate. Keep things upbeat. Laugh about life together. Be sensitive to your husband. Sure, there are things that I need to talk to Casey about, schedules to discuss, events that have happened, but I wait for the right time.

Sometimes there are heavy things that I can tell he's not up for, so I wait a few days. Now, if it's an emergency, I tell him. He's a big boy, and he'll have to handle it. But if it's something that you don't have to share right away, wait for an appropriate time.

If it's hard for you to laugh, read a joke book before your husband gets home. If you work, before you drive home with the stress of your job, think of an old movie that was just hysterical that always makes you laugh. Think of something that will bring a smile to your face.

If you work at home, change out of your sweats before he gets home. Fix your hair and apply some makeup. If you want to have a vibrant relationship, you need some life within you. You have to have a smile within you.

Sometimes when the kids were young, before Casey got home, the kids and I would hide. Then, when he walked in the door, we would say the signal, "Yoo-hoo." He had to answer, "Yoo-hoo, where are you?"

It livened him up in an instant. It's amazing what a silly game like that would do for him. Our son Caleb always popped out. Our daughter, Tasha, would become hysterical. Then there was the fact that I was hiding. He had to laugh and smile. It's way better than greeting him with, "Yeah, you're home. Guess what all happened today?"

You can't expect a perfect husband, but you can cultivate your love. You can nurture your relationship and allow him to grow in love. When you do, you'll love the results.

New Thoughts to Think

Ask the Holy Spirit to help you be more sensitive and thoughtful of your husband or wife and his or her needs. Set up a date night for two or three times a month. Read Jeremiah 18:1-6, and ask the Lord to mold you as He wills so your marriage and your sexual relationship are excellent in His eyes:

The word which came to Jeremiah from the Lord, saying:

"Arise and go down to the potter's house, and there I will cause you to hear My words."

Then I went down to the potter's house, and there he was, making something at the wheel.

And the vessel that he made of clay was marred in the hand of the potter; so he made it again into another vessel, as it seemed good to the potter to make.

Then the word of the LORD came to me, saying:

"O house of Israel, can I not do with you as this potter?" says the LORD. "Look, as the clay is in the potter's hand, so are you in My hand, O house of Israel!

8

Sound Advice for Singles of All Ages

Sometimes even Christians have a mindset so focused on our needs that we cannot, or do not, focus on God and His supply. We become needy people. This kind of needy person is the last person on earth who should get married.

I believe that this is an area where single people are especially vulnerable. You may think or feel, *I have needs, and I want a man,* or *I want a woman, and I want to be married,* and I understand that. But when you become focused on your need—whether it's fellowship, loneliness, friendship, money, sex, or something else—then you are focused on your lack.

If you enter a relationship focused on your need and lack, you have a surefire recipe for disaster. I love Casey's illustration of this.

When two people who are needy bump into each other, it's like two suckerfish who just locked lips. What happens when two suckerfish lock lips? The opposite of what happens when two blowfish lock lips.

Rather than getting bigger, two suckerfish grow smaller and eventually destroy each other. They suck the life out of one another. If two blowfish lock lips—two people who are not focused on their needs—they "blow up" or increase in size. They build each other up and help each other increase in gifts, talents, and anointings. They give life to each other.

The suckerfish scenario has happened in too many marriages. People come together because of need, and then they want their spouse to meet their need. They look to the spouse to make them feel better or make them happy. The end of this story is, when a person no longer gets their needs met in their spouse, they then look for someone new to "suck on."

So to what, or on whom, do you focus to get your needs met? You focus on your heavenly Father.

Philippians 4:19 is clear on this: "And my God shall supply all your need according to His riches in glory by Christ Jesus."

If you can see your Father as your Source to supply your every need when you are single, you will be able to see your Father as your Source when you are married. Your spouse is not your source. If you get married tomorrow, your needs remain exactly the same as they are today. Truthfully, they just doubled. Now you have to take care of a partner to whom you've committed your life.

This has to become real if you expect successful friendships, dating relationships, and a successful marriage. In every area of Christian life, whether you are single or married, when you focus on yourself, another person, on your job, company, boss, the government, the public assistance program, anything or anyone instead of your heavenly Father as the Source of all that you need, you are in trouble.

When you focus on the incorrect source, you also live a lower level of life. You experience all kinds of problems because God is really the only One who can meet all of your needs according to His riches in glory.

It's not according to the condition of the stock market, how much your company pays you, or the level of education you completed. It's not according to what the world around you says. It's according to what the Word says as in, "My God shall supply all your need according to His riches in glory by Christ Jesus."

Everything you get from God comes because of your relationship with His Son Jesus. If you don't love Jesus, embrace Him. Invite Him into your heart, and receive Him as your Savior and Lord. If you haven't, you are lost, and without Him in your life you will not be good spouse material. In that case I suggest that you stay single. If you love Jesus, then worship Him, talk to Him, read the Word daily, and trust Him.

On your first date with someone, talk about Jesus. It's not weird. If it chases the date off, you don't want him or her anyway. Be encouraged, however, that if you are single, God doesn't want you to be alone. He has a person for you. (Gen. 2:18.)

You may want to stay single, and many people do. Over the years, I have found that many choose a single life because they are afraid. They have anxieties, fears, and pain in their heart from past relationship failures or sexual issues of molestation, abuse, or promiscuity.

If you will gain God's perspective by reading God's Word and getting the truth, you'll obtain God's freedom, because truth sets you free. (John 8:32.) Then you can have the relationships, marriage, and family that God wants you to have.

When Paul told the Corinthians to stay single, he was dealing with serious issues. (1 Cor. 7:1,7.) They wanted to be sexually active all the time. He tried to get them to serve

God and renew their minds. He tried to stop them from the sin of sexual lust they were experiencing. He was not violating Genesis 2:18 where God said it is not good that a man or woman should be alone.

When he spoke to the widowed and divorced and said that it was good for them if they remain unmarried, he didn't mean forever. (1 Cor. 1:8.) His point was not to jump into another relationship immediately.

There is a theory that despite what religion has taught, it is possible that Paul was married. Paul was a member of the Sanhedrin before becoming a Christian, and I believe that the requirements for his position included marriage. If this is true, we don't know what happened to his wife. She may have left him because of his faith or maybe died at some point.[1] Either way, between that and his past of persecuting Christians, he had a lot of past to forget and a lot of future to press toward.

When he wrote in Philippians 3:12-14, "Not that I have already attained, or am already perfected; but I press on, that I may lay hold of that for which Christ Jesus has also laid hold of me. Brethren, I do not count myself to have apprehended; but one thing I do, forgetting those things which are behind and reaching forward to those things which are ahead, I press toward the goal for the prize of the upward call of God in Christ Jesus," he spoke from experience. He had authority to write that.

God has a wife or a husband for you. God said that it is not good for man to be alone, so He created a helpmate who would be perfect for you, and He wants you to find that person. (Gen. 2:18.) He wants that person to find you.

Don't become so focused on your need that you become unbalanced and weak. Stay focused on your loving, heavenly Father. He will meet all of your needs. He will supply your spiritual, emotional, mental, and physical needs. When you allow Him to do it from that point of strength, you can enter into a dating relationship, knowing your true Source, and have a wonderful time.

Don't Light a Fire You Can't Put Out

While you wait for the time when your mate comes along and you marry, it is especially important that you yield to the Holy Spirit living on the inside of you. Galatians 5:16 is very helpful: "...Walk in the Spirit, and you shall not fulfill the lust of the flesh."

It can be very hard to hold yourself in check when you date, but if you focus on walking in the Spirit, you won't fulfill the pull of your flesh. You also have to do some practical things to keep your relationship holy.

When Casey and I first started dating, he kissed me, and it made me feel different than anyone else ever had. We talked about it. We decided together to stand pure. We made a commitment not to have sex before we married. If we hadn't decided together, we wouldn't have made it. The flesh would have taken over, because no one is above the flesh.

Your actions stir up your desires. So, choose what actions you'll have. If you aren't married, don't light a fire if you can't put it out, because it is almost impossible to put out if you are single. Decide your actions ahead of time. When you become physical, your mind's ability and clarity to think *Is this the will of God for me?* flies out the window. Your flesh will take over. Then you could end up marrying someone because of guilt, condemnation, or pregnancy—instead of the destiny and will of God.

Remember, sex without marriage is fornication, which is sin. Hebrews 13:4 says that God will judge fornicators and adulterers.

Even if you intend to marry someone or are engaged, if you have sex, it is fornication. It doesn't matter whether you have seventeen days to go until the wedding date or seventeen hours; it's fornication, because you are not married.

It's like this: I want to lose ten pounds, but I haven't yet. I can't wear smaller clothes yet. If you're not married, you can't have sex yet. Once you marry, you can.

Some people say, "Oh, but we're married in our hearts," or "We're married before God." Through all the generations of time, there has been an order for mankind to go from courtship, or dating, to a covenant of marriage. Even Jesus made the distinction with the woman at the well. John 4:6-18 gives us the account:

Now Jacob's well was there. Jesus therefore, being wearied from His journey, sat thus by the well. It was about the sixth hour.

A woman of Samaria came to draw water. Jesus said to her, "Give Me a drink."

For His disciples had gone away into the city to buy food.

Then the woman of Samaria said to Him, "How is it that You, being a Jew, ask a drink from me, a Samaritan woman?" For Jews have no dealings with Samaritans.

Jesus answered and said to her, "If you knew the gift of God, and who it is who says to you, 'Give Me a drink,' you would have asked Him, and He would have given you living water."

The woman said to Him, "Sir, You have nothing to draw with, and the well is deep. Where then do You get that living water?

"Are You greater than our father Jacob, who gave us the well, and drank from it himself, as well as his sons and his livestock?"

Jesus answered and said to her, "Whoever drinks of this water will thirst again,

"but whoever drinks of the water that I shall give him will never thirst. But the water that I shall give him will become in him a fountain of water springing up into everlasting life."

The woman said to Him, "Sir, give me this water, that I may not thirst, nor come here to draw."

Jesus said to her, "Go, call your husband, and come here."

The woman answered and said, "I have no husband." Jesus said to her, "You have well said, 'I have no husband,'

"for you have had five husbands, and the one whom you now have is not your husband; in that you spoke truly."

Jesus pointed out the five times she'd been married and that she was living with someone out of wedlock. That means she had stood in the acceptable way of getting married five times and been divorced five times. Jesus very clearly defined that it's a different relationship.

If you have not made the covenant, the commitment before God and man in the acceptable fashion, in a contractual form, you are not married.

First Corinthians 6:15-18 puts it this way:

Do you not know that your bodies are members of Christ? Shall I then take the members of Christ and make them members of a harlot? Certainly not!

Or do you not know that he who is joined to a harlot is one body with her? For "the two," He says, "shall become one flesh."

But he who is joined to the Lord is one spirit with Him.

Flee sexual immorality. Every sin that a man does is outside the body, but he who commits sexual immorality sins against his own body.

One common excuse to commit sexual immortality is, "Oh, but we're going to be married in a week." Don't do it. Suppose you have sex, then later on he dies or the engagement is broken and the wedding is called off, and you get pregnant? We always believe we know what's going to happen tomorrow, but we don't. We have no guarantees.

If you have sex before marriage, you give up something very precious, and you eat the fruit of it the rest of your life. In order to protect yourself, you have to choose what actions you will engage in ahead of time. Will you kiss or not? Will you open-mouth kiss or not?

If you start down the path in the sexual area, especially if you have already experienced sex before, your desire is very real. Yes, it's God-given, but you have to pre-determine how far you will go.

It always amazes me that people who are not married ask, "How far can I go?" My question to you is "Why do you want to go so far? Why, before you know that he or she is truly the person you want to commit to for the rest of your life, do you want to go so far?"

The apostle Paul told us, "Do you not know that you are the temple of God and that the Spirit of God dwells in you? If anyone defiles the temple of God, God will destroy him. For the temple of God is holy, which temple you are" (1 Cor. 3:16,17).

I want to say to people who ask me how far they can go, "If your body is the temple of the living God, why are you so willing to 'sell' your body and your emotions so cheaply? Why 'sell' who you are—your trust, your intimacy, your vulnerability?"

You are valuable. You are a temple of the Holy Spirit. Every time you give your body away it is forever in the heart and mind of whoever you gave it to, and whoever gave it to you is always in your heart and mind.

A woman who has sex with a man to whom she is not married or committed to makes an emotional decision. You walk through your emotions of need, trust, tenderness, gentleness, and commitment.

Paul also teaches us in Romans 1:21 that when a person begins to break the laws of God, or the Word of God, their heart becomes darkened. The first time a woman has sex with a man to whom she is not married, going through all of those emotional steps and levels is a tremendous challenge. She experiences the guilt, the pain, the crying, the feelings of inadequacy, the loneliness, the emptiness, and the betrayal of her own emotions and standards.

The second time she goes through all of the same emotions, but they are slightly less. The third time slightly less again. The fourth time less again, and so on. Each time it grows less and less because her heart grows darker and darker. Finally, she reaches a place of such darkness that she is no longer in touch with the truth, and she becomes a hard shell.

No one becomes this way overnight. It happens over time. When you meet someone like this, realize it. They have given themselves so freely they've grown dark and hard, but if they would allow their heart to be touched and emotions to be felt, all those feelings of inadequacy would flood them. That list of emotions would fill them.

Darkness in giving yourself away so freely begins with insecurities, your need to belong, your need for affection, and your need to have someone believe in you and say, "You are the most valuable person to me." The desperation is so real that you willingly give yourself away for ten minutes of sex and the false feeling that these needs are met.

This happens to women of all ages and backgrounds. For Christian single women, it can take a different spin as well. I've seen single women in our church who were angry because they were "good girls." They were mad that they had not reached that level of intimacy in life. They were resentful and hid it. Eventually, this rumbling volcano was ready to erupt, but because they were Christians and in church, they hid their anger. Yet, somewhere along the way, it pops up in different ways.

I've seen women, who seemed so stable and level-headed, meet Mr. Con Man—the new guy in the church—and run off with him. They elope, get married, and then divorce a week or so later. Then the rest of the single women in the church ask in amazement, "Why did she go and do something so crazy like that?" They don't understand. That woman was mad about being a "good girl."

The other amazing part of this scenario is that men seem to have radar that can hone in on a woman like this. They are drawn to the insecurities that scream, "I need to be approved. I want to be touched. I want to be loved."

Sometimes women with these insecurities throw themselves at moral men. I've had men ask me, "What do you do when you're trying to maintain your morals in a dating relationship, and she wants to have sex? How do I turn down her invitation for sex without making her feel hurt or rejected?"

This question is good for a man or a woman. You have to choose if you are going to be a person of the Holy Spirit or if you will choose the pathway to darkness. The person you date is very likely the person you will end up marrying. How do you choose the person you date?

Choose them by their character, their values, their vision, and by what they do. If someone you date presses you to have sex, you should challenge his or her values of life. Take a stand—"That's not where I want to go. I refuse to go there. I want a person who desires to build a lifetime commitment, not someone who merely wants immediate gratification."

You have to be strong. You have to walk in the Spirit so that you will not fulfill the lust of your flesh.

Women, you have to deal with all of this in the depths of your heart. You have to deal with your feelings about being a good girl. If you're angry about it, you are unbalanced in your thinking and in your heart. You must make decisions in your heart and not just in your head.

You have to acknowledge the rumbling of the volcano on the inside of you. Acknowledge feelings that do not line up with the Word. You have to deal with it and draw on the Spirit of God for help.

Tell Him, "God, without You, I will erupt. Without You, I am unbalanced. Without You and Your Word, I am sinking fast. Help me to be strong in who I am as a woman. Help me to be pleased with who I am as a woman."

Men who give themselves away freely don't necessarily deal with the barrage of emotions that women encounter. It's not the same with men and women.

Yes, men need an emotional connection to have the fullness of what God intended, but a man can have sex with a woman and not even know her name. Emotionally, that doesn't hurt him.

It doesn't change what the sex does to his soul. God's Word is true for both men and women, and the Word says that when you have sex with someone, there is a joining to that person that forever remains. There is a connection that will affect you for the rest of your life.

How many people do you want to give yourself away to? You are a special package from God. How many people do you want to share yourself with? Every time the special package of who you are is opened, a portion remains wherever you give it.

Mom and Dad, you have to tell this to your teenagers. Don't shy away from talking about intimacy with your children. They need to hear it. They need you to be the one who talks to them about it.

Talk to them about the facts of life, including women's menstrual cycles. Tell them EVERYTHING.

I remember when our son was in a sex-education class at his school. One night we were sitting at the dinner table and he mentioned it, and Casey and I started to talk to him about it. He told us, "Oh, I heard it all at school." I quickly responded, "No, you didn't hear it all because you haven't heard it all from Mom and Dad."

They need to hear from you. Talk to them about emotional commitment. Talk to them about the exact physical things that happen. Be very real with your kids.

Sometimes when I talk to my kids, I am nervous. I giggle, but I just tell them, "Okay, I'm a little nervous, but I'm still going to talk to you." I can't let my feelings hold me back from my responsibility. I'm willing to talk about it, giggling or not.

No Ringy...No Dingy

No matter how young or how old a person is, sex outside of marriage is wrong. I've had many widowed women ask what they were supposed to do.

The answer is simple. Be disciplined. You are not supposed to put yourself in a position to be tempted. Don't go on dates to secluded places by yourself. Don't be alone with your date in your home. Don't hang all over each other or fall asleep with each other. Set up your boundaries. Make a commitment together, because one of you will be a little weaker at times when the other is stronger.

From teenagers to divorcees to widows and widowers—if there is no ring, there should be no "ding." No ringy, no dingy. There are singles who avoid sex for all the wrong reasons. They are fearful—afraid of getting pregnant, of getting caught, or of what someone will say. They are not abstaining because of a holy reverence for God and His Word.

Fear will not keep you clean. It's easy to "get around." Even if you can rationalize it in your head, if there is enough pressure from someone you care about, then they will "help" you overcome your fear, and you will have sex. Fear cannot be your motivation. It will not hold you up.

Remaining pure is hard at times, so you have to rely on the Holy Spirit to help you. You have to build up your inner man by feeding him. You do that by reading and meditating on the Word of God, confessing Scriptures, praying, going to church, listening to tapes, reading Christian books, attending Bible studies and seminars, talking about Jesus with your friends and learning from each other.

Keep yourself in the midst of what keeps you strong, what keeps your spirit man strong, so that you can resist temptation and walk in the Spirit.

Jesus said that if you believe in your heart, and say it with your mouth, you'll have it in your life. (Mark 11:24.)

The following is a confession for you to speak aloud to yourself and to God. I believe it will help you. Declare it in faith. Repeat it often. Establish your heart and your mind on the truth of God's Word. Remind yourself that He is your Source, and He is the One who will bring your mate to you.

I am a woman [or man] of God. I am living in God's will, preparing myself for the destiny He has called me to fulfill. I walk in the Word of God, the love of God, and the wisdom of God. My Father has prepared a spouse for me, before the foundation of the world. He [or she] is preparing himself [or herself] for the future we will have together. We will walk in harmony and unity all the days of our lives. Our steps are ordered of the Lord. In His way and at His time, we will meet and grow in love together. I thank You, Father, for the husband [or wife] You have for me and the great future we will share together.

New Thoughts to Think

Search your heart to ensure your actions and behavior are honest and in line with God's Word, not past hurts. If you are single, commit to staying pure. Stay beautiful on the inside for the man or woman God is preparing for you.

9

The Questions You Really Want Answered

Christians have so many questions about sex, and they don't know where to go to get the answers, or they are too embarrassed to try. I probably have been asked most of them, so I will give you the answers as honestly and clearly as I know how.

You have to have knowledge. A lack of it can destroy you. (Hos. 4:6.) You'll understand my boldness as you read these "real" questions and my answers.

Q: Is using birth control a sin?

A: The main issue with birth control methods is selecting the ones that do not cause abortions, such as IUDs, the morning-after pill, and other innovations. Stopping conception is wise in many cases. It's unwise to have an unlimited number of children if you can't pay for them or care for them or if you are not ready to have children. I encourage you to avoid getting pregnant if you don't have the finances, the home, and every means necessary to raise them properly.

Some people are raised in religions that teach, "If God wants you to have kids, it's up to the Lord." If you are having sex, most likely you are going to have children.

This question also falls under your own personal conscience. You have to check your heart and follow your decision. (John 8:9; Rom. 9:1; 1 Cor. 10:25-29; 2 Cor. 1:12.[1])

Q: Is using a condom really safe sex?

A: Using a condom doesn't change much regarding sex. It doesn't guarantee you won't get pregnant. According to what I have read, it is still possible for women whose husbands use condoms to become pregnant in the first year of typical use. If used properly, latex condoms will help to reduce, not eliminate, the risk of contracting HIV (AIDS) and other sexually transmitted diseases.[2]

As far as diseases, the only real safe sex is being married to one person all your adult life, with neither of you having sex with anyone else. (Heb. 13:4.)

Q: Should I ask my boyfriend [girlfriend], who is not a virgin, to be tested for sexually transmitted diseases before we marry?

A: Absolutely. One woman I know testified how she contracted such a disease from her husband. She was a virgin, and they had a pure dating relationship, but he had experienced sex before. She never asked him if he had until it was too late.

If you've had sex before, you should be tested whether you are in a relationship or not. You need to know, and you need to be honest with someone should it look like your relationship could develop into marriage. You don't need to tell everyone you take on a date, but if you see your relationship developing into something deeper, you need to be honest.

Even if you only had sex one time, get tested. Walk in wisdom. Saying you're just going to walk in faith concerning it is foolishness and denial. Be honest with yourself and your potential mate.

Q: My spouse wants me to wear certain kinds of clothing, videotape our sexual relationship, and use other "stuff." I don't want to. Is this wrong of me?

A: All through this book I have quoted from Hebrews 13: "Marriage is honorable among all, and the bed undefiled; but fornicators and adulterers God will judge. Let your conduct be without covetousness; be content with such things as you have…" (vv. 4,5).

Covetousness wants something you don't have that you can't earn and grow into your life. For example, if you want a new car, you can earn the money and then go buy the car, but covetousness wants something someone else has that you can't get on your own.

When you step into covetousness, you enter into a fantasy that will hurt you. If you want your wife's breasts to be bigger, you are coveting a frame she does not have. "…be content with such things as you have…."

By wanting these other "things," a person is coveting and has entered into a fantasy based on pornography he or she has read, seen on television, video, or in person, or heard from other people. Whatever the source, the spirit of it is the same. The tool or the method is irrelevant. God will still judge it.

Whether you are married or not, if you give yourself to fornication or adultery, then you are contrary to God's plan, and you open up the door for covetousness.

"I just wish my wife was taller. I wish my husband was skinnier."

Even the world can't live up to its fantasy. If your wife were a supermodel, they would still have to touch her up to put her on the cover of a magazine.

"My husband wants me to wear black and red lace and prance around and dance."

"My wife wants me to do some different things I'm not so sure about."

Neither of you is ever to make the other do or wear anything they are not comfortable with. It is wrong to coerce, push, demand, or dominate your spouse. It's always wrong to reach a place where the motivation of this world drives you.

"Well, we videotape ourselves, and then we watch it to get ourselves all stirred up."

They didn't have such equipment when the Bible was written. It's like having sex with someone else when you have to use other things to stir yourselves up.

Learn to stir each other up naturally. Start slower instead of using outside sources. Start with words of love and endearment: "This is what you mean to me. This is how I feel when I'm with you. This is how valuable you are in my life." Give your spouse a back rub. Admire that man or woman. Start with the intimacy of gentle, slow touching. Give yourself physically to each other. You'll get stirred.

If your husband wants you to put on chains, tell him, "No way." You don't do things that are destructive and foolish. You can wear beautiful nightgowns and underwear to be attractive for your husband.

Husband, consider if what you are asking her to do violates her sense of value. Are you treating her as precious? Do you recognize your wife as a treasure? Or do you see her as an item, as something to excite you?

In reality, it is the husband's job to go to the depth of the well and draw her out, to recognize her value, and to honor the marriage bed. You are to honor her as a mighty gift in your life that God has given to you.

I also believe that if a husband does things or wants sex in a way that violates the wife's conscience, if the wife will go from a "Martha spirit" to a "Mary spirit," those things can change in time. We have already discussed what those are, but if she will do that, I believe the heart of her husband will change because he is looking for abandonment. He's looking for her to give herself fully, as I discussed in Chapter 2. When a husband doesn't feel abandonment, he will begin to demand things.

Sex is not all in all. Sex is a celebration of love and commitment. Instead of being Marthas, if women will turn into Marys, they will be able to change many of the questionable situations.

"Oh, that is so naive. I've tried that." Maybe you think you tried it because you were acting like Martha saying yes with your vocal chords and no with your heart. Maybe you need to change some of those inside decisions.

A married man and woman are to be in love with one another, not in lust with one another. If you are in lust instead of love, nothing will satisfy you. You will constantly be looking for something to make your sexual relationship more exciting. As long as you are on that track, you will never be happy.

Yes, you are having sex with your spouse and not committing adultery. That's good, but if your motivation is ungodly, then there is no fulfillment.

Thoughts such as, *If she just had bigger breasts, if she would just wear this, if we could get it on video, then we could watch it once in a while,* or *If we could just do it this way,* are all lustful. They are not loving.

Thank God you are not lusting after the neighbor, but you've allowed the motivations of the world to control you, and the motivation of the world is never fulfilled.

Read the Song of Solomon in the Bible. Look at your sexual relationship from God's perspective and then from Mary's perspective.

Read 1 Corinthians 7 and Hebrews 13:4 with the mindset of the intimacy of a marriage relationship with your husband. Believe you will find freedom for many areas where you have been in bondage.

Q. Is masturbating wrong?

A: We have already covered this topic, but again, God will judge the fornicator and the adulterer.

Fornication comes from the Greek word *porneuo,* which has to do with sex outside of marriage.[3] This kind of sex has to do with sexual immorality, including pornography. Some believe that masturbation falls into this category.

In the case of young men in high school and college who masturbate, sometimes they think that when they marry, they'll stop. In my experience of years of counseling, this has not always been true. Marriage does not conquer lust. It can just be another avenue to exercise lust, in which case young men can become confused.

"I must not be in love. I used to masturbate and fantasize. I used to read sexually explicit magazines and get excited, but I thought it would all go away when I married. I thought I loved my wife. I thought I was doing God's will to get married. I must not love her like I thought. Maybe it's not God's will that we're together. She can't fulfill my life or my sexual needs. There must be something wrong with our marriage."

No, there's nothing wrong with your marriage. There's just something wrong with your motivation. You've never stopped the lust. You just transferred it into your marriage. And again, lust is never fulfilled or satisfied.

We saw earlier that when single, masturbation can damage your future marital relationship. It may cause your desire or need for a mate to diminish or dissipate. Remember, God put the desire for a sexual union in each of us. It is a driving force that propels singles toward marriage. By not allowing that desire to motivate you positively to pursue God's gift of a mate, you can greatly hinder, or even destroy, God's plan for your life.

For a married woman, masturbation may begin with fantasy that stems from watching soap operas, reading romance novels, fantasizing about having sex with someone to whom you're not married. Reality cannot compete with fantasy.

You may have had a fantasy of what Disneyland would be, and it was one long line. In the same way, maybe you had a fantasy of what your wedding would be, and it didn't live up to it.

I have been told, "Well, I can't climax if I'm not fantasizing." This is where all the fantasizing you have done in your life has brought you: Reality no longer excites you. You have to live in a sexual fantasy to climax. The motivation of what is a good marriage relationship with your spouse has now turned to bad because you cannot enjoy a normal, loving, giving relationship. You have to make it a fantasy trip.

Sir, Ma'am, you have to break these strongholds in your life. You have to renew your mind and discipline the way you think. It won't change in one night or one week, but over time you can reach a place where you love your spouse and are fulfilled without the motivation of the world.

I stated this earlier in the book, but I encourage you to go before God and repent. Allow His Holy Spirit to cleanse you on the inside, heal you, and create a new heart in you for your future. Then decide to move forward. If you are single, move forward, believing God to meet your need and bring that godly mate into your life.

Q: How do you define sex?

A: Jesus said, "If you look at a woman lustfully, you have had sex" (author paraphrase, Matt. 5:28). Well, what did He mean? Obviously, there is a difference between "We ended up in bed," and "I just looked." I've heard men say, "Well, I looked, so I might as well."

No. There is a difference. Looking is the first step. That is part of the sexual act, to look at a woman and lust for her. That leads to the conclusion, the actual act of intercourse. Both are dangerous and both are wrong.

Sex is an attitude and a physical act. It's an interaction between two people, and it can be the start or the conclusion. That's why we have to guard ourselves physically. For example, we can't go around our churches hugging each other intimately. We can hug each other as brothers and sisters in the Lord, but that's it.

Q: **Is oral sex really sex? Is it wrong or sinful?**

A: This has become such a confused issue in our society, especially among teenagers. I've read reports and watched the news as they have reported on how teens won't necessarily have intercourse. If you ask them, "Have you had sex?" they'll say, "Oh, no," but they've had oral sex a lot.

Former President Bill Clinton brought this controversy out into the open through the highly publicized scandal involving Monica Lewinsky, and our teens have suffered because of it.

Oral sex has always been sex, despite the high profile controversy surrounding it in the late 1990s.

For married couples, whether or not oral sex is wrong or sin is up to your conscience. The Song of Solomon alludes to oral sex, but there are no Scriptures specifically directed toward oral sex. Therefore, the Lord left it up to your conscience. (John 8:9; Rom. 9:1; 1 Cor. 10:25-29; 2 Cor. 1:12.⁴)

The Bible does say to flee sexual immorality and fornication. You cannot touch what isn't yours. Outside of marriage, it would definitely be sin. Inside of marriage, it should be something both husband and wife are comfortable with and agree to do.

Q: How is a person delivered from lust?

A: Begin with talking. Talking, prayer, and openness are the keys to freedom from any bondage. You cannot get free if you refuse to talk. Confession brings release. Continuing to hide brings bondage, so you have to talk to someone. It's not always a one-time talk issue. You may need continual help until you are truly free.

In most cases, you will want to talk to someone other than your spouse at first. Possibly talk to your pastor or another mature godly man, if you are a man—or another mature godly woman, if you are a woman.

In extreme cases, your pastor or mature friend may suggest that you need to get more help through ongoing counseling. Your pastor may send you to a counselor who deals with these issues all the time. I encourage you to subject yourself to their counsel. Yield to God's plan for your complete freedom.

10

Where There Is No Vision,
Attorneys Prosper

Married people need a vision for an exciting future of life together and fun together. If you can't see yourselves having fun and enjoying your marriage, work on that because where there is no vision, attorneys prosper.

Take your marriage seriously. Examine how you perceive it, think about it, and value it. God has a very high plan for your marriage. He has a great plan, and He wants to share that plan with you. Seek Him and let His thoughts and His Word renew your mind about your married relationship. Romans 12:2 says, "And do not be conformed to this world, but be transformed by the renewing of your mind, that you may prove what is that good and acceptable and perfect will of God."

There is a good, an acceptable, and a perfect will of God for your marriage. Don't settle for less than the perfect will of God. Allow the advice I have written in this book to penetrate your heart and your mind. Choose to look at what and who has shaped your thinking and your outlook on life and marriage. Address the past, confront it, talk about it honestly, and allow God to heal it.

For example, how you see men—especially your husband—is directly related to the sources of men in your life when you were growing up. Maybe you had an abusive father, or maybe there was no father present. Perhaps your parents divorced, and what was once a close relationship grew distant and awkward, thus causing abandonment and rejection.

Whatever is in your mind—your mental computer of memories—is what has shaped your thinking and your values where men and marriage are concerned.

Question your computer databank. So many things we internalize as children are evident in our thinking as adults, but we don't realize it.

If your parents divorced when you were young, you may have internalized the message, "Somehow this is my fault." If you never deal with that lie of the enemy, you will live out its effects. It's like looking through warped glass to make decisions and assessments about people and events and relationships. Consequently, you are not living in truth. You live a lie of the devil, who is only out to destroy you and those around you.

Maybe every time your dad went to hug your mom, she jerked away. You saw it repeatedly. That image is a picture in your mind, and it's a cold image. How has it affected you? How has it affected your sex life? Are you cold? Do you put little heart into your sex life? Do you coldly turn away at times, which says, "I don't trust you"?

When a message like this powerful picture is played out before you repeatedly, it sows seeds into your heart and mind. It repeatedly teaches and trains you.

God wants to input new data. He wants to put in truth, born out of the Spirit of God.

Question your thinking. Don't justify your feelings or the way you are. Go to God and invite Him in to change your heart and renew your mind. Don't let wrong programming in your computer bring destruction into your marriage and your sex life.

Our thinking is so predominant in our lives. It is the strongest force. That's why it is so critical to get God's thoughts into our minds. His thoughts are higher than our thoughts (Isa. 55:9), so we must get them—and we find them in the principles and Scriptures of His Word.

What you watched in your parents' relationship is directly linked to what you believe today. And what you believe today causes your behavior.

When you willingly look at how you think and what you believe, which explains your behavior, then you can begin to change. Then you can remove the wrong thinking and replace that now empty space with God's knowledge.

Sometimes people don't want to think of their parents' faults because they don't want to dishonor them; they don't want to accuse them. I understand that feeling, but it isn't dishonoring to reflect on your past and acknowledge human imperfection. What you recognize as wrong computer programming is personal. What you realize you internalized from your parents' behavior or communication patterns isn't something you should tell all the relatives. Don't advertise it, but let God reveal it to you and then set you free from the effects of it. If you can, discuss it with your husband or go share it with godly counsel.

Be willing to change and allow God to set you free. Then you can invite all those things that are His perfect will into your marriage, such as the things you long for—the honesty, the communication, the romance, and a good sex life.

Here's Your Homework

As you lay this book aside, take a deep breath. Now you can begin to work on your marriage. Actually, while you've been reading, your journey to a great marriage and a great sex life has already begun.

But there are some ongoing ideas I want you to hold in your heart and work on. These practical insights can help you experience lasting change. Remember:

1. GREAT MARRIAGES ARE BUILT.

Great marriages are made when each person builds in the relationship—not when one waits for the other to make a move first. Don't demand that your spouse perform before you start working on your part. Proverbs 14:1 reminds us of the truth: "The wise woman builds her house, but the foolish pulls it down with her hands."

2. FORGIVE ON A DAILY BASIS.

Ephesians 4:26 says, "…do not let the sun go down on your wrath." If you're mad or have animosity, don't go to bed until you ask for forgiveness. Don't go to sleep at night without first challenging your heart. And if you're mad at him because he didn't do what he said he would, but he doesn't know it, deal with it. If you can't get to first base with him, you still have to deal with your own heart.

Sometimes the pain may be so intense, you don't think you can take it. Maybe he didn't come home one night. You have to guard your own heart.

Proverbs 4:23 says, "Keep your heart with all diligence, for out of it spring the issues of life." If you allow unforgiveness and bitterness to fester in your heart, it will eat you up and destroy you. Write Ephesians 4:31,32 on your heart: "Let all bitterness, wrath, anger, clamor, and evil speaking be put away from you, with all malice. And be kind to one another, tenderhearted, forgiving one another, just as God in Christ forgave you."

3. PRACTICE LITTLE ACTS OF KINDNESS.

Do things the way your spouse likes them done—his breakfast or gas in her car. Place things where they like them placed. Resist the urge to act like a martyr and yield to kindness.

4. SPEAK WORDS OF LIFE EVERY DAY.

Proverbs 15:1,2 say, "A soft answer turns away wrath, but a harsh word stirs up anger. The tongue of the wise uses knowledge rightly, but the mouth of fools pours forth foolishness." Words can soothe and heal, or they can become weapons of destruction. Choose wisdom and speak words of knowledge correctly. Speak healing, restoration, and words of love.

5. Spoil Your mate with acts of thoughtfulness.

Make sweet phone calls. Leave voice mail messages. Leave cards or notes lying around. Lay his clothes out. Pull out her chair. Open the car door for her. Spoil him instead of being angry with him.

6. Touch with Love.

I love Romans 16:16. "Greet one another with a holy kiss...." The physicalness of life is real. Touching builds comfort and security. When your husband walks in the door each day, greet him with a kiss. Focus on your marriage first, regardless of what's going on around you or what has happened throughout the day. Don't be an iceberg. Don't be so focused on your own world that you forget to touch your husband. If you're afraid it will always lead to sex, practice touching more. Soon it will be touches of warmth and love, and he'll learn it doesn't have to lead to sex. Just touch his leg when you're watching TV, touch his face when you're riding in the car, squeeze his arm. Just touch him frequently.

7. Have Helping Hands.

Be quick to help. Don't always wait to be asked. Walk in the anointing of a servant as Jesus did, and serve one another.

8. Talk Politely.

Say "Thank you" and "Please." Tell him or her, "I appreciate you." For example, thank him for taking out the garbage, even if he has always done it. Just thank him for being considerate enough to take it out.

9. Look your mate in the eyes and really listen.

When your spouse talks to you, look him or her in the eyes. Listen with more than your ears. Learn to look at him or her as a person. Listen to perceive what is being said. Don't just listen with the ears so that you can hurry and say something. Stop. Slow down.

10. Give your mate space with a smile.

Give each other some space. Give one another time alone. My husband likes to clean his motorcycle and his bicycle, so I let him. I give him space to be himself. Time alone is refreshing. It quiets the noise and clamor of life and opens the door for the peace of God to come in.

11. Say Yes.

Put your husband first before the children, the career, or obligations. Someday, when the children are grown and gone, he will still be there. Be quick to go places with him. Be spontaneous. Put down what you're doing and run off with him.

12. TRUST AND COMMUNICATE TRUST.

Speak words of trust. Build a fortress of trust in your marriage. Don't let a sense of mistrust creep in just because he's ten minutes late. Quit being so fearful and gripping him so tightly. Believe in your partner and express that belief with words and actions.

13. BE IN HIS CORNER.

When your mate comes home from the job and complains about the challenges of work, don't defend his boss. Be on his side. Build him up: "I know you'll make the right choice. You'll know what to do." Wives are their husband's number one defender. If you know he's wrong, then just don't say anything, but support him. Believe in him and stand in his corner.

14. JUST LAUGH.

Laugh at what you do. Laugh at what you don't do. Laugh at life. Resist the urge to take life so seriously. If you will, then you will have a lot more fun in your life and your marriage.

Take the Risk—Mess Up Your Tidy World

If this book has agitated you, then that is good. If you are feeling vulnerable and exposed, that is good. God wants to talk to you. He wants to change your thinking, your marriage, and your sex life. He wants to visit with you about YOU. He's probably already been talking to you. So talk back to Him.

Tell Him about the issues affecting you. Resist your natural defense system that wants to move in and put walls up. Resist the urge to protect your little tidy world, where everything is placed nicely and neatly. Resist the urge to protect how comfortable you feel.

The truth is, your tiny world is too little. It's comfortable because you've grown accustomed to it, but it's too small for you. You're outgrowing it even now. This book has stirred you up. Let go. Mess up your world. The Holy Spirit is nudging you to grow and to change. He is a Gentleman; therefore, He won't pound you on the head. He will just continue to nudge you.

You can't have victory over issues in your marriage in your own strength. The issues are too big for you—and your tidy world. You need the help of the Holy Spirit. He is the Helper, so yield to Him. Allow Him to come in and rearrange your world and pull out some of the old thoughts that you've outgrown.

Let Him remove the roots that have grown in your heart over a lifetime or over the years of your married life.

Start living. Start planning the future. Dream of what a wonderful married life you can have. Plan now how to make the changes you've recognized that you need to make.

Change your thinking. Get a vision of an exciting future, of life together and fun together. Remember, if you can't see yourselves having fun and enjoying your marriage, work on that because where there is no vision, attorneys prosper.

Make plans. Plan vacations. If you can't take it this year, plan it as though you can take it next year. Plan outings. Plan overnight getaways. Plan exciting adventures. Plan homes and businesses. Get visions and dreams together. Plan what sex will be like when you can handle it. You may not be there yet, you may be a little uptight, but plan what it will be when you are free at last.

Forget that which is behind, and press on to that which is before. (Phil. 3:13.) Have a vision of the kind of marriage you want to have—not a romantic fantasy. Get a vision of good things, fun things, and positive things that you will do together. Think of serving God together, experiencing life together, seeing the world together.

When young people are dating, they talk about what they're going to do someday when they get the money or when they get married. That vision is what makes youth alive. Some older people have lost their vision and dreams. They've let the circumstances and the negatives of life lock them into some survivor mode—which means simply dying a slow death emotionally.

It's time to build great marriages in Christian homes. It's time to work hard to be good Christians who have great marriages. Then we can say to the world, "Look at us. Look at what we have. We have this because our Father has made us who we are, and we're sharing it together."

I believe that in the last days (2 Tim. 3:1-5), it won't be just the signs and wonders of healing or other miracles that attract the world. It will be the signs and wonders of marriages that last, children who are obedient, families who hang out together and enjoy each other. When we live like that, our neighbors will knock on our doors to ask, "How do you get your teenager to act like that?"

You'll answer by saying, "Well, first, let's talk about your marriage."

I'll never forget hearing of a man who went to one of our leaders in America and asked, "What are we going to do to straighten out the Congress and get the right people in office?"

The Christian leader responded, "How's your marriage?" The man was taken back. "What do you mean by that? I'm talking about the Congress of the United States of America. I'm talking about saving this country."

The man replied, "I heard your question. That's why I asked you, 'How's your marriage?' When we Christians get our priorities right, then we'll have leaders with the right priorities. As long as we don't have it, there's no way the world will ever get it."

We have to make our marriages our priorities. Husbands, love your wife. Love her as Jesus loves, and you'll find the solution to every issue and every question. Wives, submit to your husband, and you'll find the answers to every circumstance and every situation.

Husbands and wives, if you have read this book together, make the following renewed commitment together. Whether together or separately, renew your vows.

For Husbands:

I, [name], give myself to you, [wife's name], to be your husband. I receive you as my wife. Before my Father in heaven, I commit myself to be a loving, faithful husband. I will give all that I am and all that I have to you and our family. My spirit, soul, and body are committed to the success of our lives together as one.

By the love of God that is shed abroad in my heart, the faith that God has given me, and the power of the Holy Spirit, I join myself to you. I will love you as your husband and live with you as one from this day forward.

For Wives:

I, [name], give myself to you, [husband's name], to be your wife. I receive you as my husband. Before my Father in heaven, I commit myself to be a loving, faithful wife. I will give all that I am and all that I have to you and our family. My spirit, soul, and body are committed to the success of our lives together as one.

By the love of God that is shed abroad in my heart, the faith that God has given me, and the power of the Holy Spirit, I join myself to you. I will love you as your wife and live with you as one from this day forward.

Whatever the shape of your marriage and your sex life, with God you can make it better, because He can make you better. Choose to walk through the territory before you—face the unforgiveness, the pain, or the apathy. Look at this as a new day. If you need to talk to someone, go to the pastoral staff at your church—but don't let another day be stolen from you. Cling to God's Word in faith, standing and believing for your marriage and a great sex life. Remember, He wants you to enjoy great sex. So start believing that you will indeed enjoy it—from the toes up.

"Do not remember the former things, nor consider the things of old. Behold, I will do a new thing, now it shall spring forth; shall you not know it? I will even make a road in the wilderness and rivers in the desert" (Isa. 43:18,19).

Endnotes

Chapter 1

[1] *The KJV Old Testament Hebrew Lexicon,* Brown, Driver, Briggs and Gesenius, "Hebrew Lexicon entry for 'Tsela,'" http://www.biblestudytools.net/Lexicons/Hebrew/heb.cgi?number=6763&version=kjv.

[2] One example of that is in Galatians 3:28. When we receive Jesus as our Lord and Savior, that verse says there is neither male or female, but we are all one in Christ Jesus.

[3] "The woman was created, not of dust of the earth, but from a rib of Adam, because she was formed for an inseparable unity and fellowship of life with the man, and the mode of her creation was to lay the actual foundation for the moral ordinance of marriage." *Keil & Delitzsch Commentary on the Old Testament: New Updated Edition,* Electronic Database (Hendrickson Publishers, Inc., copyright © 1996). Used by permission. All rights reserved.

[4] Based on a definition from *Webster's II New College Dictionary* (Boston/New York: Houghton Mifflin Company, 1995), s.v. "join."

Chapter 2

[1] See 2 Corinthians 10:3; Ephesians 6:11,12.

[2] We apply God's Word by obeying it and speaking it over our lives.

Chapter 3

[1] "It is very likely that the skins out of which their clothing was made were taken off animals whose blood had been poured out as a sin-offering to God...." *Clark's Commentary,* by Adam Clarke, Electronic Database, copyright © 1996 by Biblesoft. All rights reserved, s.v. "Genesis 3:21."

Chapter 4

[1] A membranous fold of tissue partially covering the opening of the vagina. Based on a definition from Webster's II, s.v. "hymen."

[2] Dr. Kevin Leman, *Sex Begins in the Kitchen,* (Ventura, CA: Regal Books, copyright © 1981), p.72.

[3] Tim and Beverly LaHaye, *The Act of Marriage,* (Grand Rapids, Michigan: Zondervan Publishing House, copyright © 1976; revised edition copyright © 1998 by Tim and Beverly LaHaye).

Chapter 5

[1] Based on a definition from Webster's, s.v. "worship."

² Tim and Beverly LaHaye, *The Act of Marriage,* p 35.

³ Ibid, p. 38.

Chapter 6

¹ Based on a definition from James Strong, "Hebrew and Chaldee Dictionary" in *Strong's Exhaustive Concordance of the Bible* (Nashville: Abingdon, 1890), p. 33, entry #1993, s.v. "loud," Proverbs 7:11.

² This type of submission is "...an expression of God's ideal for marriage. The marriage relationship was designed by Him to be symbolic of the spiritual relationship between Christ and the Church...." *The Wycliffe Bible Commentary,* edited by Charles E. Pfeiffer and Everett F. Harrison, Electronic Database (copyright © 1962 by Moody Press). All rights reserved, s.v. "Ephesians 5:22."

³ Based on a definition in *Webster's New World College Dictionary,* 3d ed., (copyright © 1997, 1996, 1994, 1991, 1988 by Simon & Schuster, Inc.), s.v. "subordinate."

Chapter 8

¹ "It is not necessary to assume that Paul had never been married. Marriage was regarded as a duty among the Jews so that a man was considered to have sinned if he had reached the age of twenty without marrying...A rabbinical precept declared that a Jew who has no wife is not a man. It is not certain, but most probable, that Saul [who later became Paul] was a member of the Sanhedrim (Acts 26:10). If so, he must have been married, as marriage was a condition of membership. From 1 Corinthians 7:8 it is plausibly inferred that he classed himself among widowers." *Vincent's Word Studies of the New Testament,* Electronic Database. Copyright © 1997 by Biblesoft. All rights reserved, s.v. "1 Corinthians 7:7."

Chapter 9

¹ The context of these Scriptures is not referring to sex, but the principle of following your conscience is the same.

² Based on research done by the Centers for Disease Control and Prevention (CDC), National Center of HIV, STD, and TB Prevention, http://www.cdc.gov, "Health Topics A-Z," "A," "AIDS/HIV," "Condoms and Their Use in Preventing HIV Infection."

³ Thayer and Smith, *The KJV New Testament Greek Lexicon,* "Greek Lexicon entry for Porneuo," <http://www.biblestudytools.net/ Lexicons/Greek/grk.cgi?number=4203&version=kjv>.

⁴ The context of these Scriptures is not referring to sex, but the principle of following your conscience is the same.

About the Author

Wendy Treat is a real wife with real children and real friends, who successfully lives God's Word in a real world. Wendy received Christ into her life in 1974 and later met her husband, Casey, in 1976, while attending Bible school.

She and Casey married in 1978 and have three children. They founded Christian Faith Center in Seattle, Washington, in 1980 and continue to pastor their thriving congregation. In 1984 they founded Christian Faith School (for preschoolers through twelfth grades), where Wendy is a Bible teacher, and later Dominion College, where she is an instructor. And their daily television program, *Living on Course,* is seen by hundreds of thousands of viewers each week in the United States and abroad.

Wendy also pastors over Women's Ministries at Christian Faith Center and is a member of the Board of Elders at the church. A respected minister, she believes that a great marriage does not happen by chance—it takes great effort. Therefore, she not only loves to learn herself, but she also loves to encourage everyone she touches as she lives, preaches, and teaches God's plan for marriage and family.

To contact Wendy Treat,

write or call:

Christian Faith International
P.O. Box 98800
Seattle, WA 98198
1-888-2WISDOM (294-7366)
www.caseytreat.com

Please include your prayer requests
and comments when you write.

Prayer of Salvation

A born-again, committed relationship with God is the key to the victorious life. Jesus laid down His life and rose again so that we could spend eternity with Him in heaven and experience His absolute best on earth. If you would like to receive Jesus into your life in order to become born again, pray this prayer from your heart:

Heavenly Father, I come to You admitting that I am a sinner. Right now, I choose to turn away from sin, and I ask You to cleanse me of all unrighteousness. I believe that Your Son Jesus died on the cross to take away my sins. I also believe that He rose again from the dead so that I might be justified and made righteous through faith in Him. I call upon the name of Jesus Christ to be the Savior and Lord of my life. Jesus, I choose to follow You and ask that You fill me with the power of the Holy Spirit. I declare that right now I am a child of God. I am free from sin and full of the righteousness of God. I am saved in Jesus' name, amen.

If you have prayed this prayer to receive Jesus Christ as your Savior, or if this book has changed your life, we would like to hear from you. Please write us at:

Harrison House Publishers
P.O. Box 35035
Tulsa, Oklahoma 74153

You can also visit us on the web at
www.harrisonhouse.com

Additional copies of this book
are available from your local bookstore.

HARRISON HOUSE
Tulsa, Oklahoma 74153

The Harrison House Vision

Proclaiming the truth and the power
Of the Gospel of Jesus Christ
With excellence;

Challenging Christians to
Live victoriously,
Grow spiritually,
Know God intimately.